The Toll-houses
of Staffordshire

Tim Jenkinson
& Patrick Taylor

POLYSTAR PRESS

ISBN 978 1 907154 07 2

The Toll-houses of Staffordshire

Published by Polystar Press
277 Cavendish Street
Ipswich Suffolk IP3 8BQ
(01473) 434604
polystar@ntlworld.com

ISBN 978 1 907154 07 2

Typeset by nattygrafix

Printed by
R Booth Ltd, The Praze, Penryn

Contents

Illustrations

For

Roberta and Stan Melloy
true Staffordshire people

0.0 Introduction

Following on from four toll-house books in the West Country and four in the East of England, this one starts us off in the North of England (or from a truly northern point of view, the Midlands). As with the others, the general introductory essay is very much the same, albeit now with local Staffordshire illustrations where they have been found available. Following this the gazetteer section gives a detailed view of Staffordshire's toll-houses, including all known sites, illustrated wherever possible.

One might ask why Staffordshire? Well, co-author Tim Jenkinson, who collaborated on the Devon books, hails from Stafford town and suggested a possible venture in the Midlands, having already done some groundwork there back in 2010. This book would not have happened without his enthusiasm and energy for the project; the gazetteer entries, all the more informative for their input from Census records diligently collated by his wife Ann, fill the second and greater half of the book.

In a similar way that the Cambridgeshire book also covered a number of toll-houses on the droving routes along the waterways of that county, this volume includes a number of Staffordshire's canal toll-houses. Their story is not covered as comprehensively as we hope to have done with the turnpike roads, but they illustrate well a close similarity of purpose.

As was stated in the previous volume these books are perhaps a little ahead of their time: when the oil runs out (and rest assured that it will) there will be a wave of nostalgia for this old system of road transport, not dissimilar to that for the railways at the end of the age of steam. The Milestone Society, for which Tim is the Devon representative, is perhaps ahead of the game here and the plaque shown adjoining is at least on a surviving toll-house, rather than at the site of one.

Commemorative Plaque,
Blue Gates Toll-house,
Smethwick Cross
photo: tim jenkinson

1.0 The Turnpike Roads

Mending the Highways
(from Smith - 1970)

CAP. VIII.
The ftatute for mending of highways.

FOR amending of highways, being now both very noifom and
tedious to travel in, and dangerous to all paffengers and carriages :

(2) Be it enacted by the authority of this prefent parliament, *Who fhall be*
that the conftables and church-wardens of every parifh within *charged to-*
this realm, fhall yearly upon the *Tuefday* or *Wednefday* in *Eafter* *wards the*
week call together a number of the parifhioners, and fhall *mending*
then elect and chufe two honeft perfons of the parifh to be fur- *Surveyors*
veyors and orderers for one year, or the works for amendment *fhall be ap-*
of the highways in their parifh leading to any market-town ; *pointed for*
(3) the which perfons fhall have authority by virtue hereof, *the amend-*
to order and direct the perfons and carriages that fhall be ap- *ways.*
pointed for thofe works, by their difcretions ; (4) and the *3 Mod. 96.*
faid perfons fo named fhall take upon them the execution of *22Car.2.c.12.*
their faid offices, upon pain every of them making default, to *f. 12.*
forfeit twenty fhillings.

II. And the faid conftables and church-wardens fhall then *Four days*
alfo name and appoint four days for the amending of the *fhall be ap-*
faid ways, before the feaft of the nativity of Saint *John Baptift* *pointed for*
then next following ; (2) and fhall openly in the church the *the amend-*
next *Sunday* after *Eafter* give knowledge of the fame four days ; *ways.*
(3) and upon the faid days the parifhioners fhall endeavour *Six days are*
themfelves to the amending of the faid ways ; (4) and fhall *appointed by*
be chargeable thereunto as followeth ; that is to fay, every *5El.c.13.f.7.*
perfon for every plow-land in tillage or pafture that he or fhe *Each perfon's*
fhall occupy in the fame parifh, and every other perfon keep- *wards the*
ing there a draught or plough, fhall find and fend at every day *mending of*
and place to be appointed for the amending of the ways in that *highways.*
parifh as is aforefaid, one wain or cart furnifhed after the *18 El. c. 10;*
cuftom of the country with oxen, horfes or other cattle, and *f. 2.*
all other neceffaries meet to carry things convenient for that
purpofe, and alfo two able men with the fame, upon pain of
every draught making default, ten fhillings ; (5) and every
other houfholder, and alfo every cottager and labourer of that
parifh, able to labour, and being no hired fervant by the
year, fhall by themfelves or one fufficient labourer for every
of them, upon every of the faid four days, work and travel in
the amendment of the faid highways, upon pain of every perfon making default, to lofe for every day twelve pence. (6)
And if the faid carriages of the parifh, or any of them, fhall
not be thought needful by the fupervifors to be occupied upon
any of the faid days, that then every fuch perfon that fhould
have fent any fuch carriage, fhall fend to the faid work for
every carriage fo fpared two able men, there to labour for that
day, upon pain to lofe for every man fo fent to the faid work,
twelve pence. (7) And every perfon and carriage abovefaid *Neceffary*
fhall have and bring with them fuch fhovels, fpades, picks, *tools fhall be*
mattocks, *brought to be*

Statute for Mending of Highways, 1555
(from Serjeant & Penrose - 1973)

1.1 The King's Highway

In order to understand the turnpike road system that gave rise to toll-houses in the eighteenth century we need first to look at its origins in the mists of medieval time.

Early roads were not actual parcels of real estate set aside for the purpose of transit as have evolved today, but rather lines of least resistance where a 'right of passage' existed - the King's Highway - over ground that remained in private ownership. This still exists in vestigial form in our modern footpath network, which then as now consisted of three levels of usage: footpaths, bridleways and carriageways (now roads used as public paths). In those days diversions were implemented to maintain the right of the traveller if the road was 'founderous' or his way was blocked, rather than at the request of the owner to suit the management of the land as is now often the case.

The highway was thus a 'communal property right' available freely for the use of any subject of the Crown and as such received little or no maintenance other than out of selfish necessity to overcome a particular obstacle such as a flood or fallen tree. It was therefore in no individual's interest to invest time or money in repairing something that would mainly benefit others.

As a consequence the roads were generally in a very poor state and greatly abused by heavy loads with many horses, by spiked or narrow wheels and by the dragging of sledges or timber. Similar problems exist to this day where the selfish interest of highway users will require legislation to achieve a benefit for the common good (e.g. the limitation of motor car use), and it was indeed legislation then that was a first step on the way to improvement of the situation. A parallel can be seen here with another communal property right, that of the old strip field system with attendant grazing and hunting rights, which was also abused by selfish interest and eventually put to rights by the legislation of the Enclosure Acts.

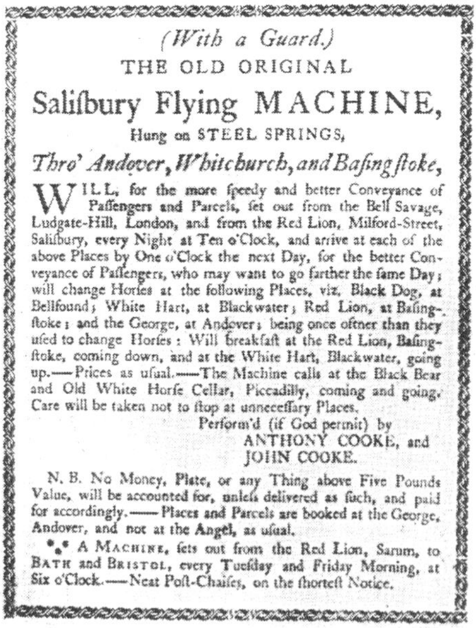

(With a Guard.)
THE OLD ORIGINAL
Salifbury Flying MACHINE,
Hung on STEEL SPRINGS,

Thro' Andover, Whitchurch, and Bafingftoke,

WILL, for the more fpeedy and better Conveyance of Paffengers and Parcels, fet out from the Bell Savage, Ludgate-Hill, London, and from the Red Lion, Milford-Street, Salifbury, every Night at Ten o'Clock, and arrive at each of the above Places by One o'Clock the next Day, for the better Conveyance of Paffengers, who may want to go farther the fame Day; will change Horfes at the following Places, viz. Black Dog, at Bellfound; White Hart, at Blackwater; Red Lion, at Bafing-ftoke; and the George, at Andover; being once oftner than they ufed to change Horfes : Will breakfaft at the Red Lion, Bafing-ftoke, coming down, and at the White Hart, Blackwater, going up.——Prices as ufual.——The Machine calls at the Black Bear and Old White Horfe Cellar, Piccadilly, coming and going. Care will be taken not to ftop at unneceffary Places.

Perform'd (if God permit) by
ANTHONY COOKE, and
JOHN COOKE.

N. B. No Money, Plate, or any Thing above Five Pounds Value, will be accounted for, unlefs delivered as fuch, and paid for accordingly.—— Places and Parcels are booked at the George, Andover, and not at the Angel, as ufual.

. A Machine, fets out from the Red Lion, Sarum, to Bath and Bristol, every Tuefday and Friday Morning, at Six o'Clock.—— Neat Poft-Chaifes, on the fhorteft Notice.

Salisbury Coach Service Poster
(from Wright - 1992)

1.2 Parish Responsibility

In the mid sixteenth century the state of the roads became of such concern that legislation was passed to firmly place the responsibility for their repair in the hands of the parish in which they were situated. The initial Act of 1555, in the brief reign of Mary Tudor, was a temporary measure which required each parish to elect two Surveyors. Their duty was to oversee the repair of roads by the inhabitants of that parish on four days per year when they were to provide 'statute labour'.

The larger landowners were also required to provide two men plus carts and tools whilst the Surveyors were permitted to dig for gravel on any waste land or commons adjoining the road. A further Act of 1562 extended the statute duties to six days per year and defaulters were liable to heavy fines.

Parishes that failed to maintain their roads properly were liable to be presented by the Justices to Quarter Sessions. If they then still failed to repair the roads satisfactorily they would be subject to indictment and the imposition of fines and/or additional days of statute labour. An occasional alternative to this was the raising of a Highway Rate by the Justices, which would then be used to pay for the necessary labour.

The problem which this system failed to tackle was that of the polluter not paying - the major users of the roads in a parish were not the inhabitants, but rather those passing through often with heavy loads for markets in other places. Their contribution to the effort of repair was made in their own parish and was but a fraction in recompense for the wear and tear they inflicted on the roads in general.

The problem of selfish interest therefore remained during a period of increasing trade in the seventeenth century and was not helped by the unwillingness of labourers (one volunteer being worth ten pressed men) nor by Surveyors whose unpaid posts were held on an annual basis and led to low levels of skill and little continuity of effort.

Pedestrian Refuges
Essex Bridge, Great Haywood
photo: tim jenkinson

1.3 Available Technology

At the end of the seventeenth century in archaeological terms, the Iron Age was still very much in progress with timber, fired clay, stone and metal being the major materials for any significant undertaking. Power was sourced from either muscle, wind or water, all three being used in the various forms of mills at fixed locations, the former two for locomotion on land or water. The wonders of steam that could turn heat into motion were as yet unheard of and the nation's wealth was traded and defended by sailing ships of timber, tar and hemp rope.

The transportation of goods thus involved considerable effort and consequently costs away from the cheapest place of production rose sharply. A number of rivers had been made navigable but significant areas remained beyond the reach of water-borne transport. The roads thus acted as both feeders to the river system and as the main means of transport where the rivers did not reach. In addition some goods did not travel well by water, others might not risk military intervention at sea whilst even more were better walking themselves to market. Whilst road transport was many times more expensive per ton per mile, the differential being relatively less for more expensive goods, it was often the preferred alternative.

There was a large network of 'carriers' operating around the country, usually based at various inns and for the most part employing packhorses. The seventeenth century saw these augmented by increasing amounts of wheeled transport, largely as a result of the increasing size and quantity of goods being traded, which led ultimately to a renewed crisis on the roads.

A response to this were the various 'Wheel Acts' which sought to limit the damage to the roads by legislating about permissible loads and wheel widths. These were doomed to failure as, essentially against the spirit of the times, they tried to contain the damage with preventative measures.

> And whereas the Wheels of many Carts, Carrs, and Brewers Drays, now commonly used for the Carriage of Goods, Beer, Ale, and other things, from place to place with in the Cities of London and Westminster, and Parishes aforesaid, where the Streets are Paved, are made thinner or narrower in the Felleys then formerly, and many are Shod with Iron Tyres, by means whereof the Pavements in the Streets of the said Cities and Places are daily impaired and broken up, and made dirty and rough: For prevention whereof for the time to come, Be it therefore Enacted by the Authority aforesaid, That from and after the Fifteenth day of December, the Wheels of every Cart, Carr or Dray to be used for the Carriage of any thing whatsoever, from any Place within the said Cities and Places, to any Place situate in the said Cities and Places where the Streets are Paved, shall be made to contain the full breadth of Six Inches in the felley, and shall not be wrought about with any Iron Work whatsoever, nor be drawn with above the number of two Horses, after they are up the hills from the Water-side; And the Owners and Pro-

Extract from London Wheel Act, 1690
(from Searle - 1930)

1.4 Justice Trusts

The parish repair system had taken each parish's previous Common Law obligation to maintain local roads and enshrined it in national legislation which was not in fact abolished until the General Highway Act of 1835. The system contained no requirement for the improvement of roads to cater for increased usage and was essentially an evenly applied remedy to a very uneven problem. Considerable differences existed between parishes both in terms of size and the numbers of roads to repair, population density and availability of labour and local geology which affected both the quality of substrate and availability of materials for repair. A further overlay of differing amounts of road usage near towns as trade increased and carriers turned to waggons and coaches led to a result that included many extremes.

In some parishes the roads were doubtless adequate whilst in others they were difficult to start with, poorly repaired and subject to increasingly heavy usage. This final straw was the key to a solution, the earliest tolls levied to pay for repair being those charged by the Justice trusts of the late seventeenth century. The first of these dates from 1663 and was set up to remedy problems on part of the Great North Road, where the Justices had previously tried all else at their disposal without success.

The concept of tolls was not new and had in the past been used to fund both 'pavage' and 'pontage' as well as to recoup costs for occasional private roads. Tolls had also been levied for markets, giving rise to a different type of toll-house in medieval times. It was therefore no great leap to apply such a toll to remedy a problem on a particular public road, the Justices retaining control of both the tolled road and the others within a parish. A further twelve Justice trusts were set up on particularly bad roads between 1696 and 1714 by which time the turnpike trust proper was beginning to emerge as a more suitable vehicle for setting the roads to rights.

Essex Bridge, Great Haywood (16th Century)   photo: tim jenkinson

1.5 Turnpike Trusts

The earliest turnpike trusts date from 1707 and, although still under the control of the Justices who were usually included amongst their number anyway, were run by trustees who were able to spread the administrative load of managing the roads which was threatening to swamp the Justices' other duties. The trusts were composed for the most part of local gentlemen and landowners, who as trustees were not able to profit from the trust itself. They could however foresee the relief afforded to their parishes by the indirect benefits of improved local economies that would ensue from making outsiders pay for the maintenance of the local roads.

Turnpike trusts were but one of many types of local 'ad hoc' body set up during the eighteenth century amongst which are included the Incorporated Guardians of the Poor. These latter set up 'Unions' of several parishes to build a workhouse, which could then be let as a going concern to a local manufacturer who would feed the occupants in return for the use of their labour, thus relieving the parishes of the burden of the poor. These were as much forerunners of local authority Social Services departments as the turnpike trusts were of Highways departments, both marking the beginnings of bringing various systems into public control, without incurring great expense.

It should be remembered that the turnpike trusts were no more than non profit making trusts set up to manage existing routes, very unlike the later canal and railway concerns which were joint stock companies with shareholders whose aim was to create new routes. Each turnpike trust was set up by an Act of Parliament, usually following vigorous petitioning by local worthies about the state of the roads. Parliamentary permission was necessary because the enterprise required the extinction of the former communal right of free passage and it became usual for Acts to last for a period of twenty one years, although renewal was usually forthcoming.

Anno XV.

Caroli II. Regis.

An Act for Repairing
the High-ways within the Counties of *Hertford*, *Cambridge* and *Huntington*.

Whereas the ancient high-way and post-Road leading from London to York, and so into Scotland, and likewise from London into Lincolnshire, lieth for many miles in the Counties of Hertford, Cambridge and Huntington, in many of which places the Road, by reason of the great and many Loads which are weekly drawn in Waggons throughthe said places, as well by reason of the great Trade of Barley and Mault that cometh

Extract from First Turnpike Act, 1663
(from Searle - 1930)

1.6 Turnpike Mania

In the years up to 1750 some 133 turnpike trusts received their Acts of Parliament and roads were turnpiked in two main areas. Firstly, and mainly before 1720, the network of radial roads emanating from London were covered by a number of linear trusts, each one's territory abutting the next. This process continued in the following thirty years alongside the second concentration of town-centred trusts which developed along the Severn valley between Bristol (at that time England's second largest city) and a rapidly developing Birmingham.

Around mid-century the turnpike idea seems to have captured the imagination in a big way and between 1751 and 1772 a further 418 Acts were passed, which effectively allowed the turnpike system to cover the country.

The uncertainties that led up to the American War of Independence brought this age of confidence to a sudden halt in 1773 and the ensuing years that also included the Napoleonic Wars saw greatly reduced activity in terms of new trusts. A further 400 or so trusts were set up between 1773 and 1836 of which 59 alone were in the years 1824 to 1826.

These later years of lesser activity were due in part to a saturation point being reached, but should also be seen against the beginnings of the years of the boom in canal building from 1770, along with the industrial revolution getting into full swing doubtless helped along its way by the greatly improved transport, trade and communications links provided by the turnpikes. The final mini-boom in turnpike activity of 1824 to 1826, probably represents a mopping up of the last remaining suitable routes in slightly improved times. Whilst Acts continued to be renewed throughout most of the nineteenth century, the last new Act of 1836 foreshadows the coming of the railways in the 1840's and the growing realisation that the days of the turnpikes were numbered.

Toll-board, Upper Wrinehill
photo: tim jenkinson

MELTON.

MESSRS. LENNY AND SMITH

Are honored with instructions from the Trustees of the Ipswich and Southtown Turnpike, to Sell by Auction,

AT THE COACH AND HORSES INN, MELTON,

ON

Monday next, October 28th, 1872

AT TWO O'CLOCK PRECISELY,

The undermentioned Valuable Properties, in Lots under such Conditions as will then and there be produced.

NAMELY. LOT 1.--The substantially erected

FREEHOLD BUILDING CALLED MELTON

TOLL HOUSE

with Shed for water carts & tools, & a large piece of excellent garden ground having a frontage upon the Main Road of about 160 feet, & another upon the Asylum Road of about 126 feet; also the toll gate & posts. LOT 2.—The materials of the Toll House at Rushmere, with the gate & posts. LOT 3.—The side gate & posts with Keepers' Hut at Kesgrave. LOT 4.—Water Cart. LOT 5.—Ditto. LOT 6.—Ditto. LOT 7.—Snow plough. LOT 8.—Wheelbarrow. LOT 9.—Ditto. LOT 10.—Ditto. LOT 11.—Ditto. LOT 12.—Pick and three stone hammers. LOT 13.—Ditto. LOT 14.—Brush bill, adze and hoe. LOT 15.—Ditto. LOT 16.—Rake and sieve. LOT 17.—Three hoes and three hammers. Also if not previously disposed of by private contract. LOT 18.—An iron pump on Rushmere Heath. LOT 19.—Ditto at Playford. LOT 20.—Two iron pumps at Kesgrave. LOT 21.—An Iron Pump at Martlesham. LOT 22.—An Iron Pump at Woodbridge. LOT 23.—Ditto at Woodbridge (near the nursery). LOT 24.—An iron pump at Melton. LOT 25.—Ditto at Melton, (next the Parish Land). LOT 26.—Ditto at Melton, (next the property of JAMES PACKE ESQ.) LOT 27.—An iron pump at Ufford. LOT 28.—Ditto at Petistree. LOT 29.—Ditto against the County Bridge at Wickham Market.

Further information may be obtained of R. B. Baas, Esq., Solicitor, and of the Auctioneers, Halesworth.

S. B. FYFE, PRINTER, HALESWORTH.

Toll-house Sale Poster, 1872
(from Serjeant & Penrose - 1973)

1.7 Winding Up

By the 1840's the turnpike road system had reached its greatest extent with over 20,000 miles of road under the control of over a thousand trusts. During the preceding century the growth and improvement of the system had greatly reduced travelling times and consequently enlarged the market place. Road construction techniques had gradually improved from the early days of simply piling another layer of gravel on top to the latter years, under the influence of great engineers like Telford or McAdam, when roads were rebuilt with a firm foundation and progressively smaller sized stones rolled in, to provide a freely draining cambered finish.

Inland transportation as a whole, with the complementary system of canals, had been greatly improved but not revolutionised, as it was still essentially bound by the limitations of muscle and wind power. It was the magic of steam in the form of the railways which ultimately brought the revolution. The turnpike system suffered first followed by the canals, as both were swept away as passengers and then freight took to the rails.

The turnpike trusts were thus subjected to falling receipts through the mid-nineteenth century which made it increasingly difficult for them to deliver the goods.

Lack of repairs led to a growing resentment to their charges amongst their customers, perhaps most strongly felt in Wales where the 'Rebecca' Riots of the 1840's saw the destruction of many gates and toll-houses by men curiously disguised in female clothing.

By the 1870's the trusts were being wound up, their assets in the form of toll-houses and equipment were sold off, and the responsibility for the roads, which they still did not own, vested in the Highway Boards, forerunners of the County Councils.

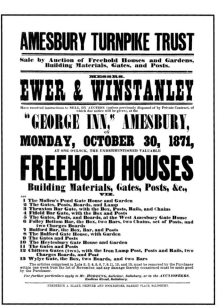

Toll-houses Sale Poster, 1871
(from Wright - 1992)

2.0 Collecting the Tolls

Toll Gate Collection
(from Smith - 1970)

A TABLE of the TOLLS payable at this TURNPIKE GATE.
[By the Local Act.]

s d

FOR every Horse, Mule, Afs, or other Beast (Except Dogs) drawing any Coach, Berlin, Landau, Barouche, Chariot, Chaise, Chair, Hearse, Gig, Curricle, Whiskey, Taxed Cart, Waggon, Wain, Timber frame, Cart frame, Dray or other Vehicle of whatsoever description when drawn by more than one Horse or other Beast the Sum of Four pence half-penny Such Waggon, Wain, Cart, or other such Carriage having Wheels of lefs breadth than four and a half inches _____ **4 $\frac{1}{2}$**

AND when drawn by one Horse or other Beast only the sum of six pence (Waggons, Wains and other such Carriages having Wheels as aforesaid) " **6**

FOR every Dog drawing any Truck, Barron or other Carriage for the space of One Hundred Yards or upwards upon any part of the said Roads, the Sum of One Penny _____ " **1**

FOR every Horse, Mule, Afs, or other Beast laden or unladen and not drawing, the Sum of Two-pence _____ " **2**

FOR every carriage moved or propelled by Steam or Machinery or by any other power than Animal power the Sum of one Shilling for each Wheel thereof _____ 1 **0**

FOR every Score of Oxen, Cows or neat Cattle, the Sum of Ten-pence and so in Proportion for any greater or lefs Number _____ " **10**

FOR every Score of Calves, Sheep, Lambs or Swine the Sum of Five pence and so in proportion for any greater or lefs Number _____ " **5**

(By 4. G. 4. C. 95)

FOR every Horse, Mule, Afs or other Beast drawing any Waggon Wain, Cart or other such Carriage having the Fellies of the Wheels of the breadth of Six Inches or upwards at the Bottom when drawn by more than one Horse, Mule, Afs or other Beast the Sum of Three-pence " **3**

AND when drawn by one Horse, Mule, Afs or other Beast the Sum of Four-Pence (Except Carts) _____ " **4**

FOR every Horse, Mule, Afs or other Beast drawing any Waggon Wain, Cart or other such Carriage having the Fellies of the Wheels of the Breadth of four inches and a half and lefs than Six inches when drawn by more than one Horse, Mule, Afs or other Beast the Sum of Three-pence three farthings _____ **3 $\frac{3}{4}$**

AND when drawn by one Horse, Mule, Afs or other Beast the Sum of Five-pence (Except Carts) _____ " **5**

FOR every Horse, Mule, Afs or other Beast drawing any Cart with Wheels of every Breadth when drawn by only one such Animal the Sum of Six Pence _____ " **6**

NB Two Oxen or neat Cattle drawing shall be considered as one Horse

3. G. 4. C. 126.

CARRIAGES with four Wheels affixed to any Waggon or Cart all as if drawn by two Horses. Carriages with two Wheels so d pay Toll as if drawn by one Horse but such Carriages are Tolls if conveying any Goods other than for Protection.

Toll Board from Sussex
(from Harris - no date)

2.1 Toll Gates & Turnpikes

The turnpike trusts were generally empowered by their Acts of Parliament to 'erect or cause to be erected a gate or gates, turnpike or turnpikes', usually in positions that were left to their own discretion. Certain towns did lobby Parliament and as a result toll-gates could not be placed nearer than three miles distant so as not to discourage local markets. Trusts with linear routes therefore tended to have toll-gates at either end of their territory with occasional others in between, often where a side road joined the way. In contrast the town-centred trusts tended to end up with a ring of toll-gates around the outskirts guarding virtually every road inwards.

The trusts were however compelled to enforce a strictly defined set of toll charges that were to a large degree proportional to the amounts of damage caused by differing types of traffic. Local traffic was often favoured by being allowed a same day return trip at no extra cost and there were a number of common exemptions from toll, notably people going to church or to vote, agricultural traffic, the Army and mail coaches which sounded their horns on approaching the gates.

Most trusts had three main employees: a surveyor to initiate and oversee repairs together with a clerk and treasurer to administer their affairs. Their tasks were to engage labour as required to mend the roads and oversee the collectors employed at each toll-gate. There was an inherent weak link in the system here that depended on the honesty of the collectors or pike-men as they became known. This led in due course to the practice of toll-farming, whereby the proceeds of a toll-gate for the coming year were sold off by auction to 'toll-farmers', either individual collectors with initiative, or contractors who took on themselves the risk of employing several collectors.

The trusts were thus assured of a toll income, which was often supplemented by composition payments from parishes who bought themselves out of their statutory labour obligations.

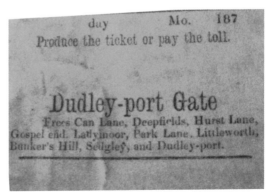

Dudley-port Turnpike Gate Ticket
photo: tim jenkinson

2.2 Toll-houses

To facilitate the twenty four hour presence of their collectors, the turnpike trusts usually built small associated dwellings at their gates:- the toll-houses. They generally comprised very minimal accommodation of two rooms with a scullery and privy attached, although larger types did become more common in later years. These toll-houses were either one or two storeyed and came in many shapes and sizes, some trusts adopting a standard design whilst others seem to have tried many variations, occasionally even an existing building, if suitably sited, being pressed into service.

If built to a normal rectangular plan they would often have gable windows very close to the front corner of the building or a bay window on the main room to provide the collector with a view up and down the road. A development of the bay came in the form of the octagonal ended house where effectively the bay became the room, this particular form becoming the norm for the toll-house building-type to such an extent that it was also employed at toll collection points on the canals. The octagonal shape also appears in some country house park gatekeeper's lodges, where again an element of control was required.

It may thus have its roots in the neo-classical love of geometry or possibly may be derived from military precedents of a defensive nature, as many toll-houses of the more ornate 'gothick' kind sport the mock battlements of the picturesque. Wherever the shape derived from, it was nevertheless of great utility and maximised the area within the dwellings for a given amount of building material. Much can be said for the presence of the buildings themselves; their many windows and forward position would undoubtedly have unsettled any approaching traveller intent on avoiding the toll with a feeling of having his every move watched. It is this presence that remains today as such a helpful clue to identifying toll-houses, particularly when they are not of the obvious octagonal type.

'Gothick' Window
Old Birchills Canal Toll-house
photo: marie marriott

Whilst the pike-man's job required his presence on the premises it was not strictly necessary for him to be on guard looking out of the windows twenty four hours of the day. Most toll-houses were built on very small parcels of land owned by the trustees, usually carved out of the corners of fields, but sufficient to allow the tenants a small cottage garden for their home grown produce. Because of their usual remoteness these small plots often also contained their own well or pump for water supply.

Internally the toll-houses would have been very cramped by modern day standards, particularly if the pike-man had a family of any size. The small bedroom would have slept the whole family, a truckle-bed for the children sliding out from beneath the main one, as can be seen at the Sussex toll-house at the Weald and Downland Museum. The other room served every other purpose, being in every sense the living room, and contained the hearth where food was cooked, together with seating, tables, storage etc. and may well have been awkward to furnish if without any square corners at all. The main door to the highway usually led off this room and it was often protected by a porch or shelter of some kind where the collector could receive tolls in the dry.

Another common indicative feature of toll-houses is a blanked out window at first floor level where a toll-board would have been placed. Sited as they were hard against the highway, those that survive today are perhaps the most visible remains of the turnpike system. The keen industrial archaeologist will also be able to find many examples of contemporary milestones, a later requirement of the turnpike legislation, as most of the roads today that show 'MS' at one mile intervals on Ordnance Survey maps were originally turnpike roads. There are also a few surviving gates, their general form consisting of a main vehicular gate or turnpike (originally a spiked pole) across the road, with usually a pedestrian gate between this and the toll-house.

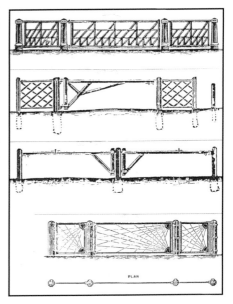

Varieties of Toll Gate
(from Searle - 1930)

2.3 Local Distinctiveness

A particular problem with toll-houses is dating their construction. In between a *terminus post quem* of the original turnpike act and a *terminus ante quem* of finding them on a tithe map or early Ordnance Survey lie many years. Most will be found to have been originally constructed nearer the earlier date at the beginning of a turnpike road's existence and therefore not benefiting from the slightly improved communications that followed by overland transport and even less likely to have benefited from the even greater improvements that the canals later brought to water borne transport.

In terms of their walling materials therefore, toll-houses were almost universally built of what was locally available and remain to this day useful pointers to local distinctiveness and the nature of the geology thereabouts. Thus in Plymouth we find the local Devonian limestone used, in Bath an Oolitic limestone, in Anglesey the local metamorphic rock and at Todmorden, in the Pennines, Millstone Grit. As eighteenth century buildings, where stone was not available, brick was usually the order of the day, so that in Cambridge we find white Gault bricks, whilst in Essex red brick and tile from the London Clay. Staffordshire will be seen to be similar with a preponderance of stone toll-houses in the north-eastern moorland area and mostly brick on the Midland plain.

Local Devonian Limestone Toll-house in Plymouth
(from Searle - 1930)

Although the timber-frame tradition had long gone into decline, and certainly was less suitable for forming an octagonal building, there is a timber-framed and thatched toll-house in Suffolk, as well as the lap-boarded Sussex example in the Weald and Downland Museum, both of which are rectangular in plan. Roofing materials show a similar pattern. Thatch was the material of an earlier age and unsuitable anyway as it represented a severe fire risk, should there be any local dissent about the coming of the turnpikes. Pantiles and the larger stone flags and tiles, whilst not best suited to the small areas of hipped roofs involved in octagonal buildings, were sometimes used nevertheless, more so on the rectangular examples.

Slate, however, was the new material of the age and seems to have been the predominant choice, even in the east where it had to be imported from afar. In the eighteenth century roofs were generally pitched according to the materials used, a slate or pantile roof requiring less timber at 30° to 40° pitch, than would a plaintile roof at 45° or more. The presence of a steep slate roof therefore often suggests a replacement covering to an earlier thatch roof.

We have seen that toll-houses were basic small domestic buildings, housing persons fairly low down the social scale. As such they fit within the vernacular tradition, although the tendency has been for them to be studied as curiosities within the province of the industrial archaeologist. Within this vernacular tradition they may be considered somewhere near its later threshold, as particularly with the octagonal forms, there is an overlay of the 'polite', a signalling of their purpose as a particular type of building. This is especially true where a standard design marks their belonging to a particular trust or they venture into the 'picturesque' at the whim of the trustees. The fashionable input could manifest itself as 'gothick' windows or even crenellated parapets, which by this time presumably no longer required the King's licence.

These fashions were however directed from above, being very much the prerogative of the trustees, who as fashionable members of the gentry would have been very aware of the latest ideas and as keen to try them out on their turnpike roads as at their lodge gates. It is therefore possible that the octagonal form used in toll-houses derived from earlier garden buildings of this shape, as is believed to have happened with park lodge gatehouses. The turnpike roads can be seen in this light as a parallel phenomenon to the enclosures and creation of our country house estates. The gentry not only came to control large areas of land, signalling this benign stewardship with their various gatekeeper's lodges, but also the routes between them.

2.4 What Lies Ahead?

Local distinctiveness relates to the customs and ways of doing things that have evolved in an area, and which give it a distinctive local character. This 'difference from other places' appears not only in the landscape moulded by our management of the land but also in our built environment. An important part of maintaining local distinctiveness therefore involves celebrating the differences, keeping alive the stories and associations of a place.

The problem with toll-houses in this respect is their situation. They were mostly built in isolation, on the perimeters of our settlements and as a consequence almost never occur within our historic centres, where most modern day celebration of place happens. Whilst the turnpikes probably initiated ribbon development, encouraging the spread of suburban villas, their remains are now largely surrounded by it, so that apart from their intimate link with the actual road, toll-houses have little sense of place.

Unfortunately the road itself has become too fast and dangerous a place to encourage anyone to stop and wonder. Meanwhile our canals and railways, which move at a more human pace, have become the subjects of the majority of transport nostalgia, and thus leisure activity.

The major residual usage of toll-houses is as dwellings and as such they are cramped and therefore often extended; they are poorly serviced because of their remoteness and often unpleasantly sited on the highway edge. We therefore find our remaining toll-houses the unconsidered remnants of a forgotten system, infrequently listed unless tending towards the more picturesque and 'polite' and severely at risk from future road developments.

In order to celebrate what is left, we need to take the first step in recognising it. Accordingly we will now look at Staffordshire's turnpike roads and toll-houses in greater detail.

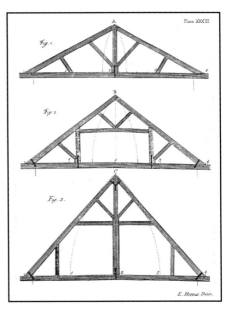

Varieties of Roof Pitch for Different Roofing Materials (from Cruickshank & Wyld - 1975)

3.0 The Staffordshire Turnpikes

Stagecoach and Four
(from Smith - 1970)

STONNALL GATE.

For every Horse or any other Beast
drawing any Coach,Chaise,Gig,or any other such
Carriage the sum of

Waggon,Wain,Cart,or other such Carriage,with
wheels of the breadth of 6 inches, the sum of......
With wheels of the breadth of 4½ inches,the sum of..
With wheels of less breadth than 4½ inches the sum of
Half the above toll payable by Oxen or Neat Cattle drawing

For every Drove of Oxen or Neat Cattle, p Score
For every Drove of Calves,Hogs,Sheep,or Lambs p Score

CASTLE-BROMWICH and HOLLAWAY-BROOK,Gates.
RICHARD SADLER, Clerk to the Commissioners.

Toll Board from Stonnall
photo: Staffordshire Arts and Museum Service

3.1 Staffordshire Turnpike Trusts

Staffordshire's first turnpike trust was granted its Act of Parliament in 1714 at the end of the reign of Queen Anne. The road in question ran from Tittensor, just north of Stone, on northwards across the north Staffordshire coalfield through Newcastle under Lyme to Talke on the county boundary with Cheshire. It was part of a longer north-south route across the county, that here followed the valley of the River Trent and was presumably in need of repair because of excessive use across a poor substrate.

The next trust came along in 1727, under George I, and covered roads north -west of Birmingham to Dudley, Wednesbury and Bilston across the south Staffordshire coalfield. The north-south route across the county was then completed in 1729 by a road from Stone in the north to Canwell Gate on the Warwickshire border and included a number of radial routes around Lichfield. Further southern coalfield routes followed around Walsall and Wolverhampton in 1748 and around Stourbridge in 1753.

The same year more out of county links were made eastwards from Tutbury via Burton upon Trent to Ashby de la Zouch in Leicestershire and to Derby from Burton upon Trent. Later in 1759 Newcastle under Lyme was also linked to Derby via Uttoxeter. In 1760, the year 'turnpike mania' really got going, a further cross-county link from Birmingham north-westwards to Chester was made, followed in 1761 by the route across the county south from Stone, this time via Stafford and Wolverhampton to Wordsley Green, just north of Stourbridge.

Sandon, just south of Stone on the Lichfield road, was connected in 1762 northwards via Leek to Bullock Smithy in Cheshire and in 1763 southwards to Stafford, later extended westwards to the Shropshire county border. Meanwhile in 1762 other small links were made with several roads on the moors around Leek in the north of the county and some roads around Dudley, Worcestershire, in the south. In 1763 a road connecting Burslem northwards to Lawton in Cheshire was sponsored by one Josiah Wedgwood, who could doubtless see the benefits of improved communications to his expanding pottery business near Stoke.

Another road across the moors came in 1765 with a link from Newcastle under Lyme north-eastwards via Burslem and Leek to Hassop in Derbyshire. Then in 1766 there came two roads south from Ashbourne, one across Derbyshire via Sudbury to Yoxall Bridge on the River Trent and the other the Staffordshire side of the River Dove from Hanging Bridges via Uttoxeter to High Bridge further west on the River Trent. Also in 1766 there were roads west from Newcastle under Lyme to Nantwich in Cheshire and from Tipton Green north-eastwards through Walsall to Muckley Corner, near Lichfield.

Further moorland roads came in 1769 from Winkhill Bank, on the Ashbourne to Leek road, south westwards via Ellastone to Darley Moor in Derbyshire and from Cheadle northwards to Butterton Moor End, extended on towards Buxton in 1770. That same year a road was added from Tunstall to Bosley in the north-west of the county along with roads around Tamworth in the south-east. In 1771 a link was added north-eastwards from Stone to Longton along with a road from Meir to Stableford Bridge, whilst in the north Shelton was linked to Cauldon eastwards across the northern coalfield.

At this point the era of turnpike mania had expired in Staffordshire and there was no further activity until 1788, when further roads around Walsall were turnpiked, followed by roads from Forsbrook to Cheddleton and from Dudley to Pattingham both in 1790. 1793 saw an east-west link made from Uttoxeter to Stone along with roads radiating from both Stafford and Sedgley further south. Cheadle and Bearsbrook, a little to its south, were both connected eastwards to Rocester on the Derbyshire border in 1799.

The 19th Century saw only a number of increasingly less important connections made within what had become by then a fairly comprehensive network. These included in 1804 roads from West Bromwich to Sutton Coldfield, and roads around Eccleshall, partly as extensions to existing trusts.

In 1807 a connection was made from Birmingham north to Shenstone south of Lichfield and in 1809 a longer route was created west from Burton upon Trent to Shirleywich on the Stone to Lichfield road. A parallel link to the same road was made in 1824 with Alrewas connected westwards to Rugeley. 1826 similarly saw Cannock connected westwards to Penkridge, whilst in 1831 a link was made northwards from Birmingham to Perry Barr. As observed by Phillips and Turton (1988), in total between 1714 and 1840 some 872 miles of road in Staffordshire were turnpiked.

Milestone, near Leek
photo: tim jenkinson

3.2 Staffordshire's Rocks

The oldest rocks with surface exposure identified in Staffordshire are the small outcrops of Silurian Limestone, perhaps 400 million year old and found around Sedgley, Dudley and Walsall north-west of Birmingham. Rocks of this age occur more generally in Mid Wales and were used in the industrial areas of Staffordshire both for lime burning and as a flux for ironstone.

Next oldest in the geological succession comes the more extensive outcrop of Carboniferous limestone around 300 million years old. This forms the hills and moors of north-east Staffordshire, effectively the southern tip of the Pennines, the backbone of northern England. It is surrounded by a ring of slightly later Millstone Grit, a coarse grey Carboniferous sandstone which once capped these hills and was much used locally for building.

Following on in the later Carboniferous are the Coal Measures from which the period takes its name, with its two coalfields in Staffordshire. The northern coalfield is centred around Stoke on Trent, the southern one running from Cannock southwards to Halesowen, west of Birmingham. In both these coalfields a central core of Lower and Middle Coal Measures is surrounded by an area of less productive Upper (and later) Coal Measures.

The rocks of the Coal Measures were also important as sources of iron ore and various good quality clays, the proximity of these to the coal providing the foundations of the Industrial Revolution that led to the two hubs of industry that now dominate the county with their two conurbations. The Coal Measures are in their turn surrounded by later rocks from the Permian and Triassic periods around 200 million years old. Each 'island' of coal is firstly ringed by a 'beach' of Keuper Sandstone, the 'New Red' sandstone as seen in south Devon and quarried for building north of Wolverhampton. The remainder of the county is pretty much a 'sea' of Keuper Marl infilling around the coalfields, this mudstone retaining the predominant sandstone red colour and defining England's midland plain with its clays good for brickmaking.

Stone walls, stone slate roof,
Goldsitch Moss, Quarnford
photo: tim jenkinson

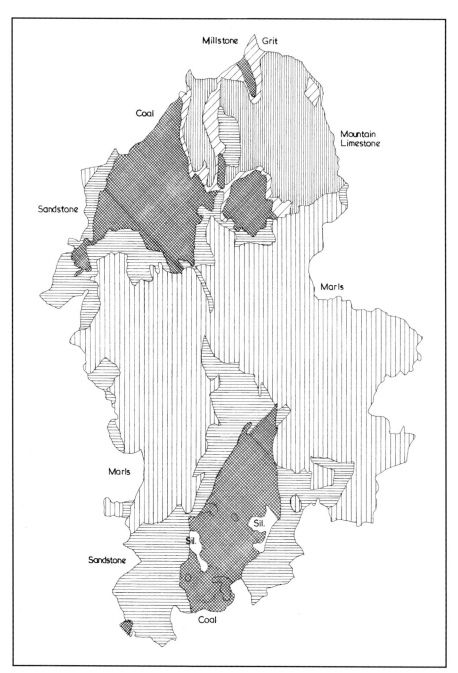

The Geology of Staffordshire

3.3 Staffordshire Toll-houses

Staffordshire's surviving turnpike toll-houses present us with a picture more akin to the counties of eastern England with mainly rectangular brick buildings of one or two storeys. The nearest to a standard design apparent here is maybe the pair from the Sedgley Trust, one now gone and the other removed to the Black Country Museum. These have an unusual design being small three bay bungalows with a high brick parapet wall hiding the pitched roof, the saved one with a square bay breaking forward.

Two quite similar large two storey rectangular toll-houses were built by the High Bridge to Uttoxeter Trust and can still be seen at Mavesyn Ridware and Middle Mayfield, effectively at either end of this trust's main route.

Two almost square two storey toll-houses, at New Road, Willenhall and James Bridge, Darlaston (demolished), also stand out for their similarity with their low pitched hipped pyramidal roofs, although they were built for different trusts.

Many of the rectangular toll-houses give a clue as to their former purpose controlling the roads with the presence of small side windows. Examples include Pipe Hill near Lichfield, Withystakes at Werrington and Scot Hay at Silverdale.

In the far north-east of Staffordshire, brick notably gives way to the local Carboniferous limestone and Millstone Grit for the toll-houses of this high moorland area at the southern end of the Pennines. Because of its relative remoteness, more of the toll-houses have survived in this area and the pages that follow have fewer text boxes than will be needed for the large conurbations where many have been lost.

Many of the moorland buildings are also a little on the small side such as at Hulme End or Goldsitch Moss, the latter employing the local stone slates for the roof.

'Picturesque' toll-house
Upper Mayfield
photo: tim jenkinson

26

Octagonal and octagonal-ended toll-houses were at one time more prevalent and were mostly brick built too, as witnessed in the wealth of old photographs unearthed during the research for this county. Two good examples survive at Upper Mayfield and Smethwick, the former with square drip moulded window heads over 'gothick' glazing, the latter with round arched window heads, more classically 'italianate' in style. Both are very much part of the picturesque tradition and have large blanked out spaces above the end windows, where their toll-boards would have been displayed.

Many of the old photographs also show toll-boards in situ along with the large lamps that permitted the business of toll-collecting to be conducted at night. The Littleworth toll-house near Stafford was at a fork in the road and appears in its illustration with toll-board, lamp and two sets of gates.

More picturesque examples of the octagonal type have survived on the canals, a selection of which are included here ranging from single storey octagonal huts (Stewpony Lock, Kinver) to three storey houses (Bratch Locks, Wombourne), this pair again 'gothick' and 'italianate' respectively. The other three storey example at Gailey Top Lock, Penkridge continues the picturesque tradition with its circular castellated parapet.

A development of the single storey rectangular toll-house had a projecting canted bay, a design much used by Telford in Scotland and also to be found in the fens of west Norfolk. Good examples in Staffordshire again survive on the canals, such as at Autherley Junction and the grand two storey version at Fazeley Junction.

It should be remembered that these canal buildings were also controlling a route and needed good all round visibility, hence their similarity to the toll-houses controlling the roads.

'Picturesque' toll-house
Blue Gates, Smethwick
photo: tim jenkinson

4.0 A Staffordshire Gazetteer

The remainder of this book comprises a gazetteer of both toll-houses and their former sites. In general all surviving toll-houses are illustrated and have a map reference without brackets. Those that have been lost are also illustrated where a suitable photograph has been forthcoming, but are given bracketed map references. The remaining toll-house sites, lost without trace other than documentary, are described as far as possible in the text boxes.

'T.P.' and 'T.G.' indicate turnpike or toll-gate as shown on the first edition 1" OS maps originating c.1809 but updated through the 19th Century (many of them showing railway routes as well). The gazetteer starts in the far south-east of Staffordshire near Birmingham in Warwickshire and runs roughly northwards through the county, ending in the north-west around Newcastle under Lyme at the borders with Shropshire and Cheshire.

The authors are very conscious of this being a first attempt to document these buildings in such detail and would be very grateful to hear of any errors, omissions, additional information or photographic evidence in respect of any toll-house that readers might be aware of. If enough new information is uncovered, a second updated edition may well be justified in due course.

Readers should be aware that most of our surviving toll-houses are now in private ownership as people's homes; please respect this. The authors apologise in advance to any owners for any nuisance this publication might bring their way, and hope the benefits of wider knowledge of this obscure subject can be seen to outweigh any inconvenience caused.

It is certainly hoped that a good many owners will come to appreciate their guardianship of this small part of our heritage, and perhaps a few more of these unique buildings will in due course get the added protection of becoming listed buildings.

Milestone, Horninglow
photo: tim jenkinson

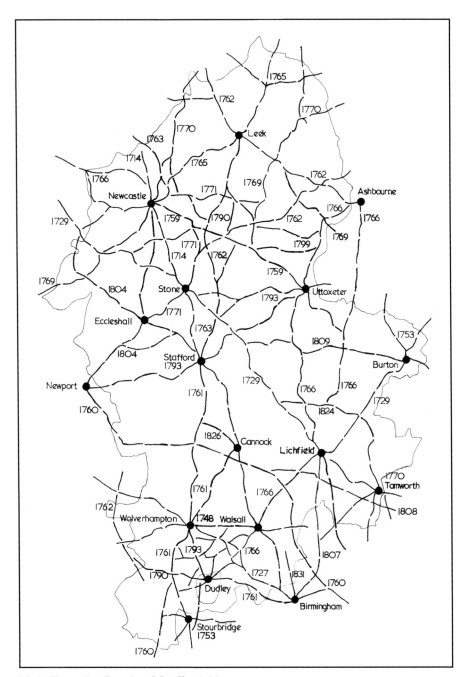

Main Turnpike Roads of Staffordshire

Date	Act	Turnpike
1714	13 A c.22	Tittensor - Talke
1727	13 GI c.14	Birmingham - Wednesbury etc.
1729	2 GII c.5	Lichfield - Stone etc.
1748	21 GII c.25	Walsall - Wolverhampton etc.
1753	26 GII c.47	Roads into Stourbridge
1753	26 GII c.59	Burton upon Trent - Derby
1753	26 GII c.85	Ashby de la Zouch - Tutbury
1759	32 GII c.60	Derby - Newcastle under Lyme
1760	33 GII c.50	Kidderminster - Wolverhampton etc.
1760	33 GII c.51	Chester - Birmingham
1761	1 GIII c.39	Stone - Wordsley Green etc.
1762	2 GIII c.42	Sandon - Bullock Smithy etc.
1762	2 GIII c.53	Kilsall - Whiston Cross etc.
1762	2 GIII c.62	Ashbourne - Leek etc.
1763	3 GIII c.45	Lawton - Burslem etc.
1763	3 GIII c.59	Stafford - Sandon etc.
1765	5 GIII c.84	Newcastle under Lyme - Hassop etc.
1766	6 GIII c.79	Ashbourne - Sudbury etc.
1766	6 GIII c.88	High Bridge - Uttoxeter etc.
1766	6 GIII c.89	Newcastle under Lyme - Nantwich etc.
1766	6 GIII c.95	Wednesbury - Bilston etc.
1766	6 GIII c.99	Muckley Corner - Wednesbury etc.
1769	9 GIII c.55	Shawbury - Newcastle under Lyme etc.
1769	9 GIII c.80	Cheadle - Butterton Moor End
1769	9 GIII c.81	Darley Moor - Ellastone etc.
1770	10 GIII c.66	Tunstall - Bosley etc.
1770	10 GIII c.99	Roads into Tamworth
1770	10 GIII c.113	Butterton Moor End - Buxton etc.
1771	11 GIII c.86	Stone - Longton etc.
1771	11 GIII c.87	Shelton - Cauldon etc.
1790	30 GIII c.100	Forsbrook - Cheddleton
1790	30 GIII c.102	Dudley - Pattingham etc.
1793	33 GIII c.131	Uttoxeter - Stone etc.
1793	33 GIII c.153	Roads into Stafford
1793	33 GIII c.167	Wombourne - Sedgley etc.
1799	39 GIII c.75	Cheadle - Rocester etc.
1804	44 GIII c.25	Ellenhall - Newport
1804	44 GIII c.40	West Bromwich - Sutton Coldfield
1807	47 GIII c.10	Birmingham - Shenstone
1809	49 GIII c.145	Burton upon Trent - Shirleywich
1809	49 GIII c.147	Soho Hill - Hamstead Bridge etc.
1824	5 GIV c.45	Rugeley - Alrewas
1826	7 GIV c.9	Cannock - Penkridge
1831	1 WIV c.47	Perry Barr - Aston / Birmingham

Main Turnpike Acts of Staffordshire

Birchfield Road Toll-house, Perry Barr
(SP 068907)
Perry Barr - Aston / Birmingham

OLD TOLL GATE PERRY BARR

photo: birmingham libraries and archives

Built on part of the Walsall Road that is now Birchfield Road at its junction with Aston Lane and Wellington Road in c.1831, this tall imposing two storey house with overhanging eaves controlled the road into Walsall from Birmingham at Perry Barr. This old photograph shows the surviving toll-board high on the wall of the house.

Recorded in 1871 shortly before the closure of the Trust the house was occupied by Nottinghamshire born 'toll-collector' William Eyre, his wife Harriet and their 13 year old son William. The toll-gates were removed in 1879 and the site today is a busy dual carriageway and roundabout on what is the present day A34.

Soho Hill Toll-house, Handsworth
(SP 053892)   'T.G.'
Birmingham - Wednesbury etc.

The Wednesbury Turnpike was set up in c.1727 along the present day Soho Road (Holyhead Road A41). At its junction with Villa Road (B4144) a toll-house once operated and became known by the name of 'Soho Hill'.

It is recorded as such in Census returns of 1861 with no fewer than three toll-collectors living at the house, the head of which being 58 year old London born 'Lessee of Tolls' Ann Walsh, assisted in the role by 40 year old lodger James Eliston and 13 year old 'servant' Edward Hunt. The toll-gates were removed in 1871.

Hamstead Road Toll-house, Handsworth
(SP 056894) 'T.G.'
Soho Hill - Hamstead Bridge etc.

photo: birmingham libraries and archives

Handsworth remained in the county of Staffordshire until as late as 1911 when it became part of the district of Birmingham. Indeed, the old village centre once laid on the road to Walsall, a route turnpiked in 1788. This two storey octagonal ended toll-house with gates either side operated at the junction of Hamstead Road with Villa Road.

This photograph taken towards the end of the turnpike era shows the toll-board positioned above the doorway. It is possible that the two figures near the door are the toll-collectors of 1871, Henry and Harriet James, then living there with their daughter Ann. Following the disbandment of the Trust in 1879 the toll-house was used as a girl's private school before being demolished at what was to become a busy road junction. To this day the name of 'Toll-Gate House' lives on in a nearby building.

Three Mile Oak Toll-house,
(SP 028902) 'T.G.' **Wednesbury**
Birmingham - Wednesbury etc.

By 1756 a toll-gate was operating at Three Mile Oak along what was to become the main Holyhead Road (A41). It was positioned a little to the east of the Hawthorns football stadium, the home of West Bromwich Albion.

In 1841 the house appears under the name of the 'Holyhead Road Toll-house' and is occupied at that time by 41 year old 'toll-gate keeper' William Welch and his family.

Blue Gates Toll-house, Smethwick
SP 019887
Stone - Wordsley Green etc.

Built c.1820 this still elegant grade II listed classically styled toll-house operated on the Dudley to Birmingham road in Smethwick, a branch of the Stone to Wordsley Green Trust's roads.

With its two storey octagonal end and blind recess with pointed arch for a toll-board above what may have been the porch and doorway, the toll-house still retains several round headed sash windows and the door appears to have been moved to the side. Probably of brick construction it is now rendered with a slate roof.

photo: tim jenkinson

Although now in the West Midlands, Smethwick was once within the boundary of South Staffordshire and is recorded as such in the Census returns of 1841. Opposite Stony Lane on the High Street, the house was once known as 'Blue Gates' a name that survives with a nearby hotel.

In the mid 1970's the house was used as a milliner's store owned by Ethel Steventon and was later renovated between 1983-4. Now bearing a blue plaque above the door showing the name of 'Smethwick Cross Toll-house' as of late 2011 it was once again looking in need of renovation.

Windmill Lane Toll-house,
(SP 027876) **Smethwick**
Stone - Wordsley Green etc.

Another toll-house operated on the main Dudley to Birmingham turnpike in Smethwick at its junction with Windmill Lane and two other roads.

Close to the nearby Cape Hill toll-gate and seemingly no longer needed, the house was eventually demolished in 1896 some 20 years or so after the end of the turnpike era in this region.

Top Lock Toll-house, Smethwick
SP 024889
Birmingham Canal

photo: tim jenkinson

This strange little brick built octagonal house is a relatively recent reconstruction adjoining Top Lock number 3 in Smethwick. It stands on a section of what is known as the Old Main Line of the Birmingham Canal Navigations (BCN) between the Engine Arm and Smethwick Junctions.

The toll-house was originally constructed in the characteristic BCN octagonal style with polychrome brickwork, a brick chimney and windows all around. In 2009 it was sadly targeted by vandals who lit fires within and as a consequence it lost its roof. Fortunately it has since been sympathetically restored.

Cape Hill Toll-house, Smethwick
(SP 035877)
Stone - Wordsley Green etc.

The main route between Dudley and Birmingham was turnpiked in 1761 and had a 'T.G.' shown on early OS maps east of Dudley at Brades Village (SO 975905).

Smethwick is on this route further east and where the road met the Birmingham boundary, there was by 1857 a toll-gate and house on Cape Hill at the junction with Grove Lane, little more than a mile east of the Windmill Lane gate.

The toll-house survived at the site until c.1925 when the coming of the motor car necessitated its demolition for road widening on this important thoroughfare. The Cape of Good Hope Hotel was subsequently built on the site.

Littleworth Toll-house, Woodsetton
(SO 939927)
Wombourne - Sedgley etc.

photo: tim jenkinson

This toll-house once stood on the north side of present day A457 opposite Holden's Brewery about 30 metres west of Vicarage Road collecting tolls for the Sedgley Turnpike Trust on the road to Tivdale from c.1845-1870.

Dismantled c.1978 and reassembled in the grounds of the Black Country Museum in Dudley the house presents as a single storey brick built cottage with projecting front section where a door and square headed window are fixed. Inside, the house is equipped with a bedroom, parlour and bathroom whilst through the back is an outbuilding, toilet and small garden.

In 1861 'toll-collector' Ellen Evans is recorded at the house, living there with her five sons in what must have been considerably cramped conditions.

Can Lane Toll-house, Coseley
(SO 935943)
Wombourne - Sedgley etc.

Built at the foot of Hurst Hill on what is the present day A463 at the point where Ettingshall road cuts Hurst Road, this toll-house collected tolls between Sedgley and Coseley at Can Lane.

It appears in the Census returns of 1861 with 33 year old 'gate keeper' Sarah Compston and her two sons in residence.

This toll-house was one of several that could be cleared in the area, if presenting a ticket from the Dudley Port Gate on the Great Bridge to Dudley turnpike.

Five Lost Coseley / Tipton Toll-houses

Wombourne - Sedgley etc.

Prince's End Toll-house, Tipton
(SO 952937 approx)
Wombourne - Sedgley etc.

Local historian Andrew Barnett cites a toll-gate at Prince's End at the eastern border of Sedgley Manor. This was an important location oft mentioned in the Turnpike Act of 1793 that sanctioned several routes out of the town to the east. The most likely place for the collection of tolls would have been around the junction of the B4163 and the A4037 between Dudley and Wednesbury. Prince's End Road appears in successive Census returns for Tipton in the mid 19th Century, but a toll-house is not recorded.

Dudley Road Toll-house, Tipton
(SO 950920)
Birmingham - Wednesbury etc.

Under a 1787 Turnpike act a section of road between Great Bridge and Dudley was extended with a branch from the Lord Dudley Arms at Trindle to the southern part of Tipton Green. The road was further extended in 1794 via Prince's End to Gospel Oak. A toll-house was built at the union of High Street with Dudley Road in Tipton where Jay's News shop now resides. It was occupied in 1871 by the 'Manager of Turnpike Roads' 35 year old James Amos, his 'toll-collector' wife Harriett and their eight year old son James junior. The toll-house probably survived at the site until as late as 1977 when it was demolished for road widening at this busy junction.

Deepfields Toll-house, Coseley
(SO 940946)
Wombourne - Sedgley etc.

This toll-house was built just east of the Birmingham Canal, close to the junction of two roads in Coseley, one leading north to Ladymoor and the other east towards Bradley. It was recorded as the 'Deepfield Toll Gate House' in 1871, then inhabited by railway porter William Smith and his family

Ladymoor Toll-house, Coseley
(SO 942952)
Wombourne - Sedgley etc.

Next in sequence after the Deepfields toll-house and about a half mile from that gate was the Ladymoor Toll. It stood in the fork of what are now minor roads branching north to Bilston and east to Bradley. In 1871 'Tailor and Toll-collector' John Harper was living at the house with his wife Harriet and 5 children.

Bradley Lane Toll-house, Bilston
(SO 955949)
Wombourne - Sedgley etc.

Probably the Bilston toll-bar described by Andrew Barnett as being on the 'Old Line', the location of this toll-house was probably at the west end of Bradley Lane at its junction with Brierley Lane. It is recorded in 1871 in the registration district of Dudley and shows 48 year old 'Toll-gate keeper' George Mansfield living there with his wife Sarah and their five children.

Bunkers Hill Toll-house, Sedgley
(SO 922935)
Wombourne - Sedgley etc.

photo: trevor genge

Another Sedgley toll-house was built on Tipton Street at its junction with Gate Street (present day A457) in the mouth of what is today Richmond Road. Known locally as 'Bunker's Hill Gate', it was recorded simply as 'Toll-gate' in 1871, with labourer William Raybold and his wife Sarah in residence.

This old photograph from c.1925 shows that the style of the house was similar to that at Woodsetton, a brick built single storey cottage with two tall chimneys, but without the projecting front section. According to Trevor Genge (1995) the house was demolished in 1933.

Gospel End Toll-house, Sedgley
(SO 914935)   'T.G.'
Wombourne - Sedgley etc.

Built at the junction of Gospel End Street and Cotwall End Road to the east of the village on the A463 the 'Toll Gate House' was occupied in 1851 by Worcestershire born 23 year old 'Toll-gate Keeper' Harriet Law, her 'tiller in iron works' husband Charles and infant daughter Catherine.
It was later occupied in 1871 by 'Labourer' Edwin Cox and his family who was probably also working as the toll-collector.

In the mid 19th Century the Sedgley Association for the Prosecution of Felons was set up to increase the efficiency of apprehending and prosecuting those committing any felony within the parish. Toll-gate keepers in the town were advised that they would receive from the treasurer a reward of one guinea (£1 1s.) for any information that led to a conviction.

Four Lost Sedgley Toll-houses

Stone - Wordsley Green etc.

Bilston Street Toll-house,
(SO 918938)   'T.G.'   **Sedgley**
Stone - Wordsley Green etc.

The first turnpike road through Sedgley was built from 1760 and ran north-south as part of the Stone to Wordsley Green Trust's routes. Built in Bilston Street c.1840 to replace an earlier toll-gate in the town centre, this toll-house stood near enough opposite St Andrew's Church and Castle Street on what is today the A463. At the time of the 1871 census the toll-house was occupied by 36 year old 'Toll gate keeper' Maria Bryan and her three children.

Moden Hill Toll-house,
(SO 920927) 'T.G.' **Upper Gornal**
Stone - Wordsley Green etc.

Marked as a toll-gate on early 19th Century Ordnance Survey maps this toll-house operated in Upper Gornal at the point where the road from Moden Hill meets the current A459 Dudley Road about a mile to the south of Sedgley. Andrew Barnett explains that the toll-house actually stood on a side road to the west.

54 year old 'Turnpike Gate Keeper' William Hartill was living at the house in 1861 with his wife and daughter Eliza as his assistants.

Shaver's End Toll-house,
(SO 924919)   **Sedgley**
Stone - Wordsley Green etc.

The Shaver's End Gate operated at what is the now the junction of the B4175 Jew's Lane with present day A459 Burton Road and Eve Lane. Recorded as Shaver's End in the Census returns of 1851 for the ecclesiastical district of St James, it stood to the south of the older Moden Hill Gate on the same road leading down into Dudley.

43 year old 'Tole Gate Keeper' John Culwick is recorded living at the house at this time with his wife Mary, whereas 20 years later 'toll-collector' John Hill, his wife and son had taken over residence.

Dibdale Road Toll-houses, Sedgley
(SO 931910 & 935910)   'T.G.' x2
Stone - Wordsley Green etc.

Two toll-houses once stood in the vicinity of Dibdale Road, one where it meets the present day B4558, half a mile north-west of Dudley, now a busy junction with a filling station, the other about a quarter mile to the west.
The former was recorded as 'Toll-gate, Sedgely' near to 'Deepdale Lane' in 1871, the latter, no doubt a phonetic interpretation by the enumerator. The inhabitants of the house at that time, were 46 year old 'Shoemaker' Joseph Cashmore, his wife Ellen and their five children. Joseph was probably doubling as the 'toll-collector'.

Askew Bridge Toll-house, Sedgley
SO 903910   'T.G.'
Dudley - Pattingham etc.

photo: tim jenkinson

Built right on the South Staffordshire border at the entrance to Sedgley Manor on Himley Road (B4176), at the junction with Brick Kiln Lane, this single storey cottage was a toll-house. It was erected c.1840 by the Dudley and Wolverhampton Turnpike Trust on what was the 'New Inns Toll Road', part of the Dudley to Pattingham turnpike.

The only surviving toll-house on its original site in the Sedgley area, it has since its turnpike days been considerably extended to the rear and is now known as 'Ednam Cottage'. The disused wooden door, once painted red, would have opened out to the road edge and is flanked by two bay windows, now with replacement frames. Recorded as the 'Himley Road Askern Bridge Gate' in the Census returns of 1871, it was occupied by 54 year old toll-collector Lydia Hale her husband John and daughter Rose.

Gornal Wood Toll-house, Sedgley
(SO 916906)   'T.G.'
Dudley - Pattingham etc.

This toll-house occasionally appears in Trust records and literature as the 'Cooper's Bank Toll-gate'. It stood near the junction of that road with the present day B4176 collecting tolls on the Himley Road for the Dudley and Wolverhampton Trust along part of the Dudley to Pattingham turnpike from 1790.

In 1871 the Census returns confirm the name of 'Gornal Wood Toll-house' but with just 30 year old 'Cordwainer' James Horton and his two year old son Joseph in residence.

39

Smestow Toll-house, Trysull
(SO 850923)
Dudley - Pattingham etc.

photo: staffordshire record office

An Act of 1790 permitted the turnpiking of the road from Eve Hill in Dudley to Himley, Smestow in Trysull and on to the New Inn in the Shropshire part of Pattingham, crossing en route the Wolverhampton to Bridgnorth turnpike, the present day A454. A toll-house was built north of the village of Smestow on what is now the B4176, at the junction of Smestow and Fearshall Roads 1½ miles west of Wombourne.

Until the 1960's, this large two storey brick built house stood at the crossroads, still known as 'Smestow Gate', and was probably the toll-house recorded at the site in

Dudley Road Toll-house,
(SO 894892) 'T.G.' **Kingswinford**
Birmingham - Wednesbury etc.

One of the Dudley and Wolverhampton Turnpike Trust toll-houses operated to the east of the village of Kingswinford on what is the present day A4101 just above the junction with Ketley Road.

It is recorded in the 1841 Census returns as in South Staffordshire at 'Bower' with 30 year old 'collector of tolls' James Lewis living there with his wife Jane and their three young children.

successive mid 19th Century Census returns for Trysull. In 1861 'Agricultural labourer and toll-gate keeper' Joseph Muchall is at the house with his wife Elizabeth and their six children. Ten years later Sussex born 'Toll-gate collector' John Norris had taken over the role living there with his wife Elizabeth and niece Lucy Parsons.

Stewpony Lock Toll-house, Kinver
SO 861848
Staffs & Worcs Canal

photo: tim jenkinson

Dated 1772 above the doorway this small single storey part octagonal grade II listed toll-house at Stewpony Lock stands on the main Staffordshire and Worcestershire Canal at Kinver and collected tolls from boat traffic for that company.

The attractive house overlooks lock no. 13 on this stretch of canal between Stourport and Stourton and it retains a central octagonal chimney stack. The door faces the canal and there are recessed round arched windows to the side.

In 1851 Birmingham born Mary Edwards is recorded as the toll-collector living in the house with her husband William.

Halfcot Toll-house, Kinver
(SO 868857)   'T.G.'
Kidderminster - Wolverhampton etc.

An Act of 1760 allowed for the road running north from Kidderminster into Staffordshire at Whittington near Kinver to be turnpiked with a stretch beyond to join the Wordsley Green to Wolverhampton road south of Himley.

Shown as 'T.G.' on early OS maps 'Halfcot' is a long lost name for an area north of Stourton on the Wolverhampton Road (A449) just south of Prestwood.

Tolls were being collected there in 1861 by 69 year old Kidderminster born Thomas Cook, living there with his wife Hannah. By 1871 the toll-house built by the Dudley and Wolverhampton Turnpike Trust had become known as the 'Halfcutt Toll Gate' with 'Boot and shoemaker' Edwin Badger and his family in residence.

Lost Stourbridge area Toll-houses

Roads into Stourbridge

New Wood Toll-house, Stourton
(SO 874850)   'T.G.'
Roads into Stourbridge

About as far south-west as you can go in the county of Staffordshire, this toll-house was recorded in 1861 as the 'Stourton Toll-gate' occupied by 28 year old 'Toll-collector' Eliza Palmer, her 'coal miner at iron works' husband William and their two young children.

It was built c.1816 on what is now the A458 by the Stourbridge and Bridgnorth Turnpike Trust close to where the course of an old Roman Road once crossed about a mile to the east of Stourton near New Wood. The house actually appears under the name of New Wood in the 1871 Census with 60 year old 'toll-collector' Edward Wise living there.

Brettell Lane Toll-house,
(SO 903861) 'T.G.' **Kingswinford**
Roads into Stourbridge

The 1861 Census records 'Toll-gate keeper' William Eyre, his wife Eliza and son William Warner at this toll-house, shown as 'T.G.' on early 19th Century maps at the east end of Collis Street.

Another 'T.G.' is shown nearby at SO 896856 to the south of the junction of Brettell Lane with the present day A491 Stourbridge road, at Platts Crescent near the western end of Collis Street in what is now the district of Amblecote.

Stone - Wordsley Green

Bromley Lane Toll-house,
(SO 890880) 'T.G.' **Kingswinford**
Stone - Wordsley Green etc.

Shown as a 'T.G.' on early 19th Century maps this toll-house was built on the road to Stourbridge on the present day A491 at the junction of Stream Road and Bromley Lane. Built under an Act of Parliament from 1761 by the Stone to Wordsley Green Turnpike Trust it was along with the tollgates at Wordsley and Amblecote, one of three to operate on this road between Kingswinford and Stourbridge.

High Street Toll-house,
(SO 893867) 'T.G.' **Wordsley**
Stone - Wordsley Green etc.

Shown as a 'T.G.' on what is now the A491 near its junction with the B4180 going east into Brierley Hill this toll-house also appears in the Census of 1871.
It was recorded as the 'High Street Toll Gate House' with 'toll-collector' John Larcombe his wife Mary Ann and their 14 year old niece Susan Bond living there.

Quarry Bank Toll-house,
(SO 928864)   'T.G.'   **Brierley Hill**
Stourbridge - Cradley etc.

A branch off the Stourbridge to Halesowen road, northwards into Staffordshire, had a toll-gate at Quarry Bank, shown as 'T.G.' on early OS maps.

Bratch Locks Toll-house, Wombourne
SO 867938
Staffs & Worcs Canal

photo: tim jenkinson

Dating from around 1772 when the Staffordshire and Worcestershire Canal was constructed by James Brindley, this fine looking grade II listed red brick toll-house stands at Bratch Locks near Wombourne in South Staffordshire. Three storeys in height, the house possesses two doors one on the higher level adjacent to the side road and bridge and the other at the lower level where the toll-keeper would emerge to greet barge owners about to use the unique staircase of locks here.

Recorded as the 'Lock House, Bratch' in the parish of 'Wombourne Orton Liberty' in the 1851 Census, it was occupied at that time by 45 year old 'Cheque Clerk' Thomas Jackson, his wife Hannah and their four children.

Wall Heath Toll-house	Fighting Cocks Toll-house,
(SO 883903) 'T.G.'	(SO 917966) **Wolverhampton**
Stone - Wordsley Green etc.	*Stone - Wordsley Green etc.*

Wall Heath Toll-house
(SO 883903)   'T.G.'
Stone - Wordsley Green etc.

A 'T.G.' is shown on what is now the A449 half a mile south of the turn to the village of Himley near Kingswinford, at or near the junction with a side road to grade II listed Holbeche House which is now a privately owned care home.

Holbeche is famously associated with the last stand of the Gunpowder conspirators of 1605 who were either shot at the house or captured and later executed.

Fighting Cocks Toll-house,
(SO 917966)   **Wolverhampton**
Stone - Wordsley Green etc.

The road leading south from Wolverhampton to Birmingham via Sedgley and Dudley was first turnpiked in 1761. Taking its name from the then nearby Fighting Cocks Inn, a toll-house stood at the intersection of Wolverhampton Road East (A459) and Goldthorn Hill Road (A4039).

Local historian Andrew Barnett advises that the road running south to Sedgley was once known as Streetways. Appearing as the 'Wolverhampton Road Toll-house' in 1871, 'Toll-collector and shoemaker' Andrew Narrowmore was living there with his wife Elizabeth.

Penn Road Toll-house, Wolverhampton
(SO 904968)   'T.G.'
Wednesbury - Bilston etc.

photo: wolverhampton journal

This fine looking traditional two storey octagonal toll-house with arched gothick windows was built at what was then the foot of Coalway Lane in Penn Road and replaced the gate that had stood at the bottom of Poole Street in Wolverhampton on the Wednesbury to Upper Penn turnpike.

It appears under the name of the 'Penn Fields Toll-house, Upper Penn' in the Census returns of 1871, when 64 year old Rachel Morgan and her 25 year old daughter Anne are recorded as the 'toll-collectors'. Marked as a 'T.G.' on OS maps from the 1830's at 'Cold Lanes' the house

Catchem Corner Toll-house,
(SO 932965)   'T.G.'   **Ettingshall**
Wednesbury - Bilston etc.

The road between Wednesbury and Upper Penn was turnpiked in 1766.

Marked as a toll-gate on early 19th Century Ordnance Survey maps, the house at the appropriately named 'Catchem Corner' stood about a mile east of the 'Fighting Cocks Gate' close to the junction of what is present day Parkfield Road (A4039) and Manor Road (A4126) in Ettingshall.

controlled the road running south of the then town through Upper Penn to Himley and Kingswinford on what is the present day A449. Still standing in 1905 it was captured at that time in the photograph above in an article on the old toll-gates of Wolverhampton and District in the Wolverhampton Journal.

Gibbet Lane Toll-house, Bilston
(SO 936972)　　　'T.G.'
Walsall - Wolverhampton etc.

Another of the Wolverhampton Turnpike Trust's toll-gates controlled Bilston Road in Priestfield near the junction of what is now Stow Heath Lane and Ward Street on the present day A41.

The two storey toll-house with octagonal end is recorded in the Census returns of 1841 as the 'Gibbett Lane Toll-Bar' with 25 year old 'Contractor of tolls' George Miles in residence.

By 1881 the house still retains that name, but is then occupied by 'Cement Stone Dealer' William Perry and his family after the Turnpike era had ended.

This old photograph shows its proximity to the road edge with a space on the front wall above the doorway that once supported a toll-board.

photo: wolverhampton archives and local studies

Gospel Oak Toll-house, Tipton
(SO 967943)　　　　'T.G.'
Birmingham - Wednesbury etc.

This toll-house once stood at the junction of Gospel (A4037) and Wednesbury Oak Roads in the Tipton district at the eastern extremity of Sedgley Manor. That said the house cannot be located in the Census returns of the mid 19th Century so may have been known by another name.

A Turnpike Act of 1793 sanctioned the building of roads around Sedgley, the longest of which being the stretch from Wombourne to the Wolverhampton to Birmingham turnpike at Gospel Oak.

Four Lost West Wolverhampton Toll-houses

Walsall - Wolverhampton etc.

Newbridge Row Toll-house,
(SO 894998)   **Tettenhall**
Walsall - Wolverhampton etc.

Described in the Wolverhampton Journal in 1905 as being on the Tettenhall Road and 'a few yards this side of the canal bridge', the toll-house is recorded in 1841 as the 'Newbridge Row Toll-house' with 25 year old Henry Howell his wife Sarah and their sons James and George in residence.

The toll-house probably stood on that part of the A41 just south-east of the Staffordshire and Worcestershire Canal in Newbridge and was in existence for some time after the start of the old horse trams in Wolverhampton. An 1837 watercolour painting of Tettenhall Rock by Robert Noyes, showing the toll-gate beyond, is held in the William Salt Library in Stafford.

Horsehill Toll-house,
(SO 893987) **Wolverhampton**
Walsall - Wolverhampton etc.

This house is described in 1905 as being at the bottom of what is now Richmond Road on the route west out of Wolverhampton towards Compton. This would place it at or near the junction of a minor road leading south to present day Merridale on what is now the A454 to Bridgnorth in Shropshire.

The toll-house was one of three toll-gates set up on this road in the mid 19th Century and it appears in the Census returns of 1871 as the 'Compton Road Turnpike House' with 55 year old 'toll-collector John Taylor living there.

Compton Toll-house
(SO 884987)
Walsall - Wolverhampton etc.

The only reference found to this toll-house is also in the Wolverhampton Journal article of 1905, when it is described as having operated at the bottom of the hill at Compton on a road leading south to Finchfield.
This places the toll-house quite close to the village, near the junction of what is today the B4161. It was one the Trust's later toll-gates set up on this road as it is not shown as a 'T.G.' on early 19th Century OS maps.

Chapel Ash Toll-house
(SO 906987)   'T.G.'
Walsall - Wolverhampton etc.

Built on the Tettenhall Road at Chapel Ash this toll-house and gate controlled access into the town from the north and west along what is now the A41 from Newport in Shropshire.

It was built in the fork of three roads about a mile or so out of the town and is marked as 'T.G.' on early OS maps, operating on a turnpike that dates from 1748.

Wrottesley Road Toll-house, Wolverhampton
SJ 878004
Walsall - Wolverhampton etc.

A Turnpike Act of 1748 permitted the build of a section of road from Wolverhampton through Tettenhall to the Wergs and thence through Wrottesley towards Shifnal at the county boundary.

The original route passed along what is present day Wrottesley Road before improvements sanctioned under an Act of 1810 took the course of what is now the A41 to Newport.

This quaint grade II listed two storey building stands amid a much larger complex in Wrottesley Road.

Still known as 'Toll Cottage' and possibly linked to the old turnpike here, it is only its position, set well back from the road, that brings into question this claimed former role.

A toll-house at Newbridge Row built not long after the new road was completed would have superseded the older gate here.

photo: history and heritage

Stafford Road Toll-house, Wolverhampton
(SO 913999)   'T.G.'
Stone - Wordsley Green etc.

In 1761 an Act of Parliament was passed to build an improved route between Stone and Wordsley Green in Kingswinford, passing through both Stafford and Wolverhampton. The first toll-gate north of the latter was originally positioned at the bottom of Lower Stafford Street, but later moved to near where the railway bridge crosses the road (A449), this point shown as 'T.G.' on early 19th Century OS maps.

Also known as the 'North Road Gate', the toll-house was demolished soon after the end of the turnpike era and replaced by a large building at the entrance to the Great Western Railway Institute, but unfortunately many years later this too suffered a similar fate.

Top Lock Toll-house, Wolverhampton
SO 918990
Birmingham Canal

photo: tim jenkinson

Prior to taking up his position at Hednesford Wharf in 1905 'Canal toll-collector' Tom Pearce, his wife Annie and their six children were living at the Lock House just off Southampton Street in Wolverhampton.

It is probable that this is one of the two grade II listed houses still surviving in a small terrace beside the lock on the Birmingham Canal.

Now known as 'Top Lock Cottages' the most likely is the one with a large bay window at the centre point (number 109) complete with lantern above illuminating what would have been the doorway opening out on to the towpath by the lock.

Bilston Road Toll-house,
(SO 923981) 'T.G.' **Wolverhampton**
Walsall - Wolverhampton etc.

The turnpike between Wolverhampton and Wednesbury dated from 1748 and a toll-house was subsequently built in Bilston Road. Shown as 'T.G.' on early OS maps it was one of a pair toll-gates set up on the road into Bilston by the Wolverhampton Turnpike Trust, the other being at Gibbet Lane in the 'New Village' of Priestfield.

Occupied in 1861 by 52 year old 'toll-collector' Septimus Newcombe and his wife Mary, this toll-house stood on what is now the A41, near a point where Commercial Road once joined.

Autherley Junction Toll-house, Oxley
SJ 901021
Staffs & Worcs Canal

photo: tim jenkinson

Opened to boat traffic in 1835 Autherley Junction is the point where the Shropshire Union Canal terminates and the Staffordshire and Worcestershire Canal begins at Oxley two miles to the north of Wolverhampton.

This grade II listed elegant single storey toll-house with a projecting octagonal bay set back from the canal retains a huge central brick chimney that seems to be rather out of character with the rest of the building.

Probably contemporary with the junction build, the toll office operated for the Staffordshire and Worcestershire Canal Company, charging tolls in accordance with a predetermined gauging measure that assessed how low each boat was in the water along with the type of cargo they were carrying.

Gorsbrook Toll-house, Bushbury
(SJ 913005)
Stone - Wordsley Green etc.

This toll-house once stood on the Wolverhampton side of the then Oxley Manor Lodge in Stafford Road at the foot of Oxley Bank in Gorsbrook. A rather late addition it was the second of two close together toll-gates on this route north out of the town along what is today the A449.

Nothing remains of the house or lodge at this point today, indeed Oxley Manor itself shown on early 19th Century OS maps was demolished in 1929. In the Census of 1871 the 'toll-bar keeper' is recorded as 45 year old Emma Summerfield living there with her husband William and their two children.

Four Lost North Wolverhampton Toll-houses

Stone - Wordsley Green etc.

Cannock Road Toll-house
(SJ 927001)   'T.G.'
Stone - Wordsley Green etc.

The first toll-gate on the Cannock Road, present day A460, stood on the corner of a crossroads leading north to what was Rumballows Farm and south to The Heath, now Heath Town, little more than a mile from Wolverhampton.

Shown as a 'T.G.' on early OS maps it fails to appear in successive Census returns of the mid 19th Century and may have like the gate at nearby Newbolds been superseded by then by the house at Bickford's Harbour on the corner of Bushbury Road.

Horseley Fields Toll-house,
(SO 927984) 'T.G.' **Wolverhampton**
Walsall - Wolverhampton etc.

A toll-house and gate once operated at little more than half a mile from Wolverhampton at the junction of Lower Horseley Fields (A454) and Lower Walsall Street on the approach to Moseley along the road to Willenhall.

Marked as 'T.G.' on early 19th Century OS maps it was one of a ring of tollgates positioned around the town at that time.

Westcroft Toll-house, Bushbury
(SJ 940028)   'T.G.'
Stone - Wordsley Green etc.

Another 'T.G.' is shown on early 19th Century Ordnance Survey maps on the Wolverhampton to Cannock turnpike (present day A460) at a turn to Westcroft one mile or so to the south of Featherstone.

This was the third in a line of toll-gates on this route in relatively quick succession.

Bickford's Harbour Toll-house,
(SJ 930008)   'T.G.'   **Bushbury**
Stone - Wordsley Green etc.

'Bickford's Harbour' was an area of arable meadow and pasture land bounded by the road leading from Wolverhampton to Cannock.

Marked as a 'T.G.' on early OS maps near Newbolds, the 'Toll Bar' was occupied in 1861 by 56 year old 'Iron maker' Clive Merry, his wife Mary and no less than ten other members of their family.

A toll-house is said to have stood on the corner of Bushbury Road that was still in evidence in 1905, having been moved south to the junction from an earlier position at SJ 929011.

Gailey Top Lock Toll-house, Penkridge
SJ 920104
Staffs & Worcs Canal

Built c.1800 at Gailey top lock on the Staffordshire and Worcestershire Canal this grade II listed toll and lock keeper's house is known locally as the 'Roundhouse' because of its distinctive appearance, that would have facilitated the toll-keeper's view of the approaches to the lock.

Standing just a short distance from the Watling Street (A5), it is three storeys high with a castellated roof and is nowadays used as a small shop for travellers stopping off at the lock. In 1861 the house is recorded in the parish of Calf Heath, Hatherton with 49 year old 'canal toll-collector' John Cowan, his wife Caroline and their eight children in residence.

photo: tim jenkinson

Three Tuns Toll-house, Oxley
(SJ 913026)
Stone - Wordsley Green etc.

A later addition to the Wolverhampton Turnpike Trust's toll-gates along the road to Stafford, present day A449, stood at what was the Three Tuns in Oxley, at the junction of a minor road leading east to Bushbury.

It appears in successive Census returns as the 'Oxley Toll-Gate', occupied in 1871 by 38 year old 'Toll-gate keeper' Elizabeth Milton her 'painter' husband Edward and their two sons Harry and James.

Town End Toll-house, Penkridge
SJ 929140   'T.G.'
Cannock - Penkridge

Marked as a toll-gate 'T.G.' on early 19th Century OS maps, this rather plain and indistinct building known as 'Old Tollgate Cottage' stands about half a mile out of Penkridge on the B5012 towards Cannock, close to where the road bridge straddles the Staffordshire and Worcestershire canal at the Wharf, shortly before the route loops back to join the A449.

The turnpike here dates from an Act of 1826 that linked Cannock on the Stafford - Churchbridge route to the southern end of the town. The two storey house has few distinguishing features to confirm its status and it is perhaps only the name and position that nowadays suggest its one time involvement in the collection of tolls. Described as a timber-framed house in Cannock Road, it was occupied in 1871 by 45 year old 'toll-gate keeper' Elizabeth Tooth from Colwich.

photo: tim jenkinson

Ivetsey Bank Toll-house,
(SJ 830107)   'T.P.'   **Blymhill**
Chester - Birmingham

A 'T.P.' is shown on early 19th Century OS maps on Watling Street (A5) on the approach to Blymhill Road a quarter of a mile west of Ivetsey Bank.

Nothing remains at the site today apart from a grass triangle on the north side of the road at the turn towards the village.

Rodbaston Toll-house, Penkridge
(SJ 914114)   'T.G.'
Stone - Wordsley Green etc.

Long swept away by road widening on the present day A449 during the 1930's, a toll-house once stood close to the junction with the road to Rodbaston Agricultural College near Lane Farm where 'Mile Houses' now stand.

Built by the Stone, Stafford and Penkridge Trust and known as 'Rodbaston Gate' on part of the 1761 Stone to Wordsley Green turnpike, it was occupied in 1871 by 33 year old 'toll-collector' Jane Oakley, her husband James and their four children.

Cocksparrow Lane Toll-house, Penkridge
(SJ 961116) 'T.G.'
Cannock - Penkridge

Shown as a 'T.G.' on early 19th Century OS maps, this classically styled two storey octagonal toll-house, known locally as the 'Round House', once stood two miles from Cannock at the junction of Cocksparrow Lane with the New Penkridge Road, now B5012. The road here was constructed in 1826 to link Penkridge with the industrial towns of Walsall and West Bromwich. The house itself was built in 1828 and took £70 worth of tolls in its first year.

photo: museum of cannock chase

It was recorded as the 'Tolegate House, Cannock Road' in the Census returns of 1861 with 23 year old 'farmers labourer' Frederick Belcher, his wife and young son in residence.

Brick built with a central chimney the house had a large space above the doorway for a toll-board and probably a porch at one time to the road edge. Reported upon in 1960 as being still in evidence at the eastern boundary of the Parish of Penkridge, it stood empty for many years and was demolished a short time thereafter for road widening at the junction.

Four Crosses Toll-house, Hatherton
(SJ 954095)
Chester - Birmingham

The road between Chester and Birmingham was divided into four districts under a Turnpike Act of 1760 with a branch extending from Newport in Shropshire through Weston under Lizard and Ivetsey Bank to Stonnall. Another of the Watling Street toll-houses was built on the present day A5 at Four Crosses, where roads go north to Hatherton and Cannock and south to Calf Heath and Shareshill.

It later appears in turnpike records as the 'Hatherton Toll-house' collecting tolls for the Cannock Trust. It was occupied in 1861 by 34 year old 'Toll contractor' William Woodhouse, his wife Charlotte and two year old Comfort Williams a visitor. Upon the demise of the Trust the house is said to have been incorporated into the fabric of the Four Crosses public house that in 2014 is currently closed and up for sale.

Wharf Toll-house, Hednesford
(SK 000112)
Birmingham Canal

photo: cannock chase heritage trail

Purpose built in 1905 by the Birmingham Canal Navigations Company on part of the Cannock Extension Canal at what was then Hednesford Wharf, this large two storey house was occupied by Dudley born canal toll-clerk Tom Pearce, his wife Annie and their eleven children until Tom's retirement in the 1930's.

The basin here, overgrown on the right of this photo, was used by the nearby East Cannock Colliery to transport coal to the Black Country until the mine's closure in 1957. This section of the canal itself closed in 1963 due to subsidence and was subsequently drained, the

Bridgtown Toll-houses, Cannock
(SJ 985085 & 984083)   'T.G.' x 2
Chester - Birmingham

Two toll-gates operated in that part of Cannock now known as Bridgtown, at either end of Bridge Street. One was about a mile south of the town on what is now the A34 and the other at the junction of Bridge Street with Watling Street (A5).

Both toll-houses appear as 'T.G.' on early 19th Century OS maps but neither could have survived the expansion of industry and road widening that has taken place here in the 20th Century.

toll-house being demolished sometime thereafter. Today at the start of the 21st Century part of the area is known as the Old Hednesford Park and is a popular open space to the south of the town.

New Road Toll-house, Willenhall
SO 963984
Walsall - Wolverhampton etc.

photo: marie marriott

A new road was built through the heart of Willenhall c.1818 to improve passage between Walsall and Wolverhampton at a time of great industrial growth in South Staffordshire. Unfortunately it ran through an area known as 'The Shrubbery' that had up until that time been an expanse of unspoilt countryside greatly enjoyed by local people.

A two storey square built toll-house operated on the new turnpike and survives today as a florist's shop opposite a large supermarket. Now part incorporated into a bigger building at the side the toll-house retains some of its original features such as a doorway facing into a side road with a gothick arched window above. Easily overlooked in this busy town, it is remarkable that it has withstood the passage of time and the industrial developments of recent centuries.

Wedge's Mills Toll-house,
(SJ 966081) 'T.G.' **Cannock**
Stone - Wordsley Green etc.

The road between Cannock and Wolverhampton was first turnpiked in 1761. A 'T.G.' is shown on OS maps about a mile to the south of the Watling Street (A5) near the village of Wedge's Mills.

A nearby pub retains the name of 'Chase Gate' that may relate to the former toll-house here. Appearing under the name of 'Wedge's Mills' in the Census returns of 1841, the 'toll-gate keeper' at that time was 55 year old Mary Henshaw living there with 15 year old Mary Carpenter.

Walsall Road Toll-house, Willenhall
SO 968986
Walsall - Wolverhampton etc.

photo: marie marriott

This most attractive two storey mock timber-framed building has been used as a restaurant for over 45 years. Now 'Ye Olde Toll-house' in Walsall Road, Willenhall, it once operated on the turnpike from Walsall to Wolverhampton, originally built in 1750. This toll-house would have worked in conjunction with the one in New Road .

Standing on the south side opposite present day Russell Street, it presents us with a traditional octagonal ended building that has been extended to the rear. The porch would have once edged into the road where a doorway now remains below a mock gothick window at first floor. A large brick chimney has been dismantled since its toll-collecting days.

Great Wyrley Toll-house,
(SJ 993072) 'T.G.'   **Cannock**
Muckley Corner - Wednesbury etc.

The road between Walsall and Churchbridge was turnpiked in 1766. A toll-house stood in Great Wyrley on what is the present day A34 Cannock to Bloxwich Road, at the junction with a side road leading to Landywood.

Marked as 'T.G.' on early 19th Century OS maps, the toll-house was occupied in 1861 by Liverpool born 'Gate keeper and Toll-collector' Daniel Unsworth, his wife Ann, their three young children and Daniel's brother in law John Meadon.

Dangerfield Lane Toll-house, Darlaston
(SO 975955)   'T.G.'
Wednesbury - Bilston etc.

photo: darlaston local history group

This classically styled, brick built, two storey octagonal toll-house survived at this site at the top of Dangerfield Lane until 1903. Originally built by the Bilston Turnpike Trust in c.1826, it replaced an earlier toll-gate that had existed since the time of the build of a new road from Upper Penn in Wolverhampton through Moxley to join the Holyhead Road to Wednesbury some fifty years earlier.

In the Census of 1851 it appears under the returns for 'Monway Field, Wednesbury' with 33 year old Welsh born 'Coal Miner and Tollgate Keeper' Thomas Edmonds in residence with his wife Lavinia and their two young children.

Moxley Toll-house, Darlaston
(SO 969959)   'T.G.'
Wednesbury - Bilston etc.

At around the same time as the original toll-gate was set up in Dangerfield Lane in c.1776 another toll-house was built in the newly formed Moxley Road to Bilston near its junction with Holyhead Road and is shown as such on early 19th Century maps.

This toll-house completed a quartet of collecting points around Darlaston and was occupied in 1851 by 'Turnpike Gate Keeper and Labourer' William Turner, his wife Ann and their two children, along with two other family members and 30 year old lodger Charles Madeley.

James Bridge Toll-house, Darlaston
(SO 989974)　　'T.G.'
Muckley Corner - Wednesbury etc.

photo: walsall local history centre

Photographed here in around 1937, this two storey square brick built toll-house once stood on the north side of Darlaston Road, present day A4038, at the west end of James Bridge. Marked as 'toll-gate' on early 19th Century OS maps it collected tolls on the road into the town from the direction of Walsall.

In 1861 the 'James Bridge Toll-house' was occupied by 50 year old 'Collector at the Turnpike Gate' Ellen Finlay, her two Railway Clerk sons and teenage daughter Mary. By 1871 the building is listed as a former toll-gate house indicating the closure of the Trust. Still standing as late as 1965 the house was demolished not long thereafter, a victim of bridge strengthening and straightening of the road at this point.

Breakback Hill Toll-house,
(SO 978964)　'T.G.'　**Darlaston**
Wednesbury - Bilston etc.

A new road out of Darlaston towards High Bullen in Wednesbury was opened in 1787 by the Bilston Turnpike Trust that maintained 11 miles of road between the towns. It was built across open land and included a stiff and unpopular climb up Kings Hill which became known locally as 'Breakback'.

Marked as a 'toll-gate' on old maps a toll-house was built at the foot of the hill little more than half mile out of town. This may be the 'Darlaston Road Toll-house' that is referred to in Turnpike Records but as it seems not to be recorded in the mid 19th Century Census returns it may have been abandoned by that time.

Sutton Road Toll-house, Walsall
(SP 022979)
Walsall - Wolverhampton etc.

photo: w f blay

This two storey cottage was built in Sutton Road to replace the Woodend toll-house and according to Blay (1932) stood 'beyond the boundary wall of the 'Shrubbery' and was positioned on the corner of Princes Avenue not far from the Crescent. In 1861 the 'Toll-gate keeper' is recorded as 33 year old Letitia Summer living there with her 'locksmith' husband Henry and their four children. The house was demolished in the 1870's.

Blay recounts a charming story that a young boy went to fetch a pig in a barrow along Sutton Road but when he reached the toll-gate two pence was demanded for the passage of the pig. Having no money on his person, the boy was forced to leave his scarf 'in pledge' and had it returned to him the following day when he paid the two pence toll.

Woodend Toll-house,
(SP 019980)   **Sutton Road**
Walsall - Wolverhampton etc.

A toll-house was built in 1748 at the junction of what was then known as the Woodend Turnpike (now Sutton Road) and Peakhouse Road (now Birmingham Road) in a place still called Six Ways. The Woodend toll-gate was later moved to the corner of Princes Avenue in Sutton Road at SP 022979.

According to Blay (1932) all persons passing or re-passing through Woodend should pay a toll notwithstanding that they had paid a toll at any other gate, but they were not subject to the payment of tolls more than once on any day.

Three Lost Walsall Toll-houses

Muckley Corner - Wednesbury etc.

Sneyd Wharf Toll-house,
(SJ 985019)   **Bloxwich**
Wyrley & Essington Canal

Tolls were once collected from a house at Sneyd Wharf near Sneyd Lane in Bloxwich on a section of the Wyrley and Essington Canal.

Known locally as the 'Curly Wyrley' because of its undulating course, the canal ran from Wolverhampton to Huddersfield Junction near Lichfield.

In the Census returns of 1891 'Sneyd Villa' is occupied by 23 year old 'Canal Toll-collector' Thomas Welch, his wife Ada and his 82 year old grandfather Thomas Cooper.

Blakenhall Lane Toll-house,
(SK 003013)   'T.G.'   **Bloxwich**
Muckley Corner - Wednesbury etc.

A Turnpike Act of 1766 permitted the build of a lengthy stretch of road between Muckley Corner through Rushall and Walsall to Bescott Brook and from there to Wednesbury via Wood Green. From there the road extended to Lea Brook and on to Toll End at Ocker Hill and then passed over Horseley Heath to Tipton Green along part of the Great Bridge to Bilston Turnpike.

Shown as a 'T.G.' on early 19th Century OS maps a toll-house was built just to the north of the Blakenhall Lane junction with what is the present day B4210 that runs north through Bloxwich towards Cannock and Great Wyrley.

Flax Oven Toll-house, Stafford Street
(SP 010995)   'T.G.'
Muckley Corner - Wednesbury etc.

The road to Cannock was turnpiked in 1766 and an original toll-gate first operated at the junction of Blue Lane East and Portland Street (SP 009991) and by 1824 it had become known as the 'Flax Oven Gate' due to its position near fields where flax was grown (Blay 1932).

A new toll-house was built c.1845 further along Stafford Street to the north to manage the junction with Profitt Street and the then Deadman's Lane, present day Hospital Street, but the house continued to be known by the name of the earlier gate.

Old Birchills Toll-house, Walsall Top Lock
SP 004994
Wyrley & Essington Canal

photo: marie marriott

A quaint single storey toll-house not far from the road at Old Birchills in Walsall once operated at the Top Lock on a section of canal that was opened in 1841 in order to provide a link between the town's canal and the Wyrley and Essington branch. Now grade II listed, the toll-house retains three distinctive gothick windows on its octagonal end that would have provided good views in both directions.

In 1871 it appeared in the Census returns as 'Birchills Lock House' occupied at that time as indeed for the past twenty years by long standing toll-collector 55 year old Abel Jones and his wife Alice.

Holloway Bank Toll-house, Hill Top
(SO 992937)   'T.G.'
Birmingham - Wednesbury etc.

The original Turnpike Act for the road between the city of Birmingham and Wednesbury in South Staffordshire dated from 1727. A toll-house was subsequently built on what is today the A4196 at Hill Top roughly half way between Wednesbury and West Bromwich. It stood a little way to the north of present day Witton Lane on Holloway Bank.

Marked as a 'T.G.' on early 19th Century OS maps it was used to collect tolls for the Birmingham and Wednesbury Turnpike Trust until its demise in 1870.

Four More Lost Walsall Toll-houses

Muckley Corner - Wednesbury etc.

Cartbridge Lane Toll-house,
(SP 021998)   **Rushall**
Muckley Corner - Wednesbury etc.

A replacement for the nearby Butts Lane Gate in the early 19th Century, this toll-house was built at the junction of what is now Cartbridge Lane with the main Lichfield Road from Walsall.

This may be the building recorded as the 'Prutte Tole-house Lichfield Road' in the 1861 Census, with 'Toll-collectors' Samuel and Jane Wilkinson living there with their four children.

Rushall Toll-house,
(SK 028011)   'T.G.'
Muckley Corner - Wednesbury etc.

A 'T.G.' is marked at the junction of several roads in the centre of Rushall on the present day A461 about one mile north east of Walsall town centre.

Nothing discernable remains at the site today but in 1841 the house was nonetheless occupied by 30 year old 'toll-collector' Isaac Taylor his wife and four children.

Wood Green Toll-house
(SO 995958)   'T.G.'
Muckley Corner - Wednesbury etc.

A toll-house operated on the road between Wednesbury and Walsall, the present day A461, at Wood Green on part of the then Muckley Corner to Tipton Green Turnpike first sanctioned under an Act of 1766. There was also a toll-bar across the end of Brunswick Park Road on the old road from Wood Green to Birmingham.

The toll-house is shown as 'T.G.' at or near the junction of Hobs Road and Rooth Street near the gateway of 'Myvod House', once the residence of William Lloyd MP. It was occupied in 1861 by 68 year old 'toll-collector' John Coleman and his wife Lucy and was according to Blay (1932) demolished around 1868 to become part of the Myvod grounds.

Butts Lane Toll-house, Walsall
(SP 019993)   'T.G.'
Muckley Corner - Wednesbury etc.

According to Anne French (2003), Butts Gate formed the boundary between Walsall and Rushall. Although the road through Walsall towards Lichfield was originally turnpiked in 1766 it was not until 1831 that Lichfield Street was built.

Before that the main route out of Walsall was along Rushall Street and into Ward Street. A toll-gate operated in what is now part of the road that ran through Walsall Arboretum where the lake now is. Present day Butts Street joins the road at the old lodge and side entrance to the arboretum. This gate was later replaced further to the north at Cartbridge Lane upon completion of the new road.

Birmingham Road Toll-house, Walsall
(SP 025973)
Walsall - Wolverhampton etc.

photo: w f blay

Blay (1932) explains that this two storey toll-house was built c.1815 near the junction of present day Birmingham Road and Broadway (present day A4148) but was not used for collecting tolls until the Woodend Turnpike Gate ceased to function.

It is described by the author as a 'good specimen of a Georgian dwelling, retaining its porch with a window on each side of it, giving an outlook up and down the road'.

Following the end of the turnpike era in 1872 the toll-house was purchased

Town End Toll-house, Walsall
(SP 010987)
Walsall - Wolverhampton etc.

A toll-gate and house once operated in the vicinity of the junction of Townend with the Wolverhampton Road close to the centre of Walsall.

Originally turnpiked in c.1748 the road between the two towns was greatly improved through Willenhall in c.1818.

by Henry Bruce who had it demolished and rebuilt in Gillity Road close the entrance of a lane leading to Gillity Fields. This is the position it occupies in the photograph above, where it was known as 'Mayfield Cottage' until its demolition sometime post 1930's.

Hilton Toll-house, Shenstone
SK 077053
Muckley Corner - Wednesbury etc.

photo: marie marriott

A complicated network of roads was turnpiked under a 1766 Act of Parliament, the longest section following a convoluted route between Muckley Corner and Tipton Green, via Walsall, Wednesbury and over Horseley Heath.

About a mile south-west of Muckley Corner, this elongated two storey house stands on the corner of Pouk Lane near the village of Hilton, off the main Lichfield to Walsall route (A461). Muckley Corner on Watling Street is about a mile to the north-east and Pouk Lane threads its way north-west to meet the main road.

Now 'Tollgate Cottage', implying a role in the turnpike era, this is not confirmed by turnpike or Census records, but it

Muckley Corner Toll-house,
(SK 083065)   **Brownhills**
Muckley Corner - Wednesbury

Muckley Corner on Watling Street was an important turnpike location where several roads converged. A toll-house operated just east of there from c.1814 along with a side bar at nearby Moat Bank.

As a result it appears in the 1861 Census returns under the name of 'Side Bar House, Pipe Place, Wall' and was occupied by 26 year old 'Toll-gate keeper' Mary Ann Wells and her four year old son George.

would have been in a convenient position to catch travellers attempting to evade tolls at the Rushall toll-gate by travelling via Aldridge.

Anchor Bridge Toll-house, Brownhills
(SK 053048)   'T.G.'
Chester - Birmingham

photo: walsall local history centre

A two storey toll-house with angled front once stood at Anchor Bridge in Brownhills on the present day A453 Chester Road, about a quarter of a mile from the Shire Oak. This old photograph shows it to have been brick built with a tall chimney, space above the doorway for a toll-board and possibly a porch that has been removed from the front.

It collected tolls from travellers moving between Cannock and Walsall through what was an important coal mining district in the mid 19th Century. In 1861 the house is recorded as the 'Catshill Toll-house' and at that time the enumerator reported that it was 'not slept in'. It was demolished in 1910 during widening of the Chester Road.

Ogley Toll-house, Brownhills
(SK 045065)   'T.G.'
Watling Street Roads

This toll-house once stood in the vicinity of the Hussey Arms on Watling Street (A5). Sections of this Roman Road that runs through the heart of the Brownhills district were turnpiked under a late Act of 1808 (48 GIII c.65).

Recorded under the name of the 'Ogley Toll-gate' in the 1861 Census returns, 42 year old 'Toll-gate Keeper' and widow Ann Duxbury was at the house at that time, living there with 12 year old 'visitor' Ellen Prixton.

Four Lost Toll-houses near Lichfield

Lichfield - Stone etc.

Elmhurst Toll-house, Lichfield
(SK 106131)   'T.G.'
Lichfield - Stone etc.

The road from Lichfield to Handsacre was turnpiked in 1729 and by 1766 a toll-house had been built where Featherbed Lane becomes Tewnall Lane (A515). In 1830 a side-bar was erected here and a new toll-house built where Tewnall Lane leaves the road to Handsacre (B5014). The toll-house stood near the point where Seedy Mill Lane joins the main road not far from the present day Lichfield Golf and Country Club, that was opened in 1991.

In 1871 the 'Toll-Gate House' is recorded in the Parish of Curborough and Elmhurst and at that time was occupied by 28 year old 'Farm servant' Edward Boston, his wife Emma and their son Charles aged 6. It survived at this point until the 1940's, when it was demolished for road widening.

Cleat Hill Toll-house, Longdon
(SK 090128)   'T.G.'
Lichfield - Stone etc.

On the road between Lichfield and Rugeley (A51) this toll-house collected from travellers at Cleathill about half a mile south of Longdon Green at point where a section of old road now loops to rejoin the main thoroughfare.
In 1851 the house was occupied by 72 year old 'Toll-gate keeper' George Wilson and his wife Elizabeth.

Streethay Toll-house, Lichfield
(SK 142105)
Lichfield - Stone etc.

The main route from Lichfield to Burton upon Trent was turnpiked in 1729 via Burton Old Road on part of the Roman Ryknild Street. A toll-gate was set up near Manor House on what is now the A5127.

It is recorded in the Census of 1871 as 'Toll-gate House, Streethay' with 44 year old 'toll-collector' Mary Knight there with two teenage daughters. It seems that the old toll-gate lodge was built on the west side of the road in 1767 and survived at the site until its demolition in the 1940's.

Freeford Toll-house,
(SK 133084)   **Whittington**
Lichfield - Stone etc.

Known locally as the 'Freeford Gate', this toll-house was less than a mile from the centre of Lichfield on what was the Tamworth turnpike, present day A51. Close to the Horse and Jockey public house and Dean Wharf, today the pub survives whilst the toll-house became a victim of road widening.

'Toll-collector' Mary Hadman, her husband John and their four young children are recorded at the house in 1871, whereas ten years earlier the lone occupant had been 60 year old 'toll-collector' Charlotte Gaskell.

Pipe Hill Toll-house, Lichfield
SK 093080   'T.G.'
Lichfield - Stone etc.

photo: tim jenkinson

The Lichfield to Walsall road was turnpiked in 1729 and a toll-house had been built in the hamlet of Pipe Hill by 1787. Enlarged in 1827, it is probable that this now whitewashed building on the A461 just south of the crossroads is the toll-house in question. Of two storeys and now known as 'Toll-Gate', it has been heavily overbuilt and extended to the side and rear, but does retain a small roadside window perhaps indicative of its former role.

Situated about two miles from the city centre, the toll-house was occupied in 1851 by 39 year old 'Toll-gate keeper' John Morris and 11 year old 'house servant' Samuel Reynolds. The Lichfield turnpike era ended in 1879, when the toll-gates were taken down.

Woodend Toll-house, Shenstone
(SK 110019)
Birmingham - Shenstone`

A toll-house once stood in the village of Shenstone Woodend on the present day Birmingham Road (A5127) which was the Lichfield to Sutton Coldfield turnpike dating from 1807. The most likely site is at or near the point where Footherley Lane joins the main route.

The house is recorded in various turnpike records as positioned opposite Pool Meadow and it appears in the Census of 1871 as 'Wood End' with 53 year old 'toll-collector Catherine Bailey in residence with her 'labourer' husband James.

Stonnall Toll-house, Shenstone
SK 075025
Chester - Birmingham

photo: tim jenkinson

Built on the Chester Road (A452) beside a lane to Gainsborough Hill Farm around 1759, it is probable that one of these two storey cottages that have been greatly extended to both the sides and rear was the house that was known in the turnpike era as the 'Stonnall Gate'.

Recorded in 1861 as 'Toll-Gate House, Thornall Common, Lower Stonnall' it was occupied at that time by 71 year old 'Toll-gate keeper' William Simmons, his elderly wife Ann and their 13 year old granddaughter Harriett.

Remarkably the old toll-board from this house survived for many years and can be seen on page 21.

Sutton Coldfield Toll-house
(SP 121970) 'T.G.' **(Warwicks)**
Birmingham - Shenstone

Shown as a 'T.G.' on early 19th Century OS maps this toll-house was built c.1807 half a mile north of Sutton Coldfield at the junction of Lichfield and Tamworth Roads.

Sutton once lay on an important turnpike from Birmingham along the Lichfield Road as far as Watford Gap whereupon the road became the responsibility of the Lichfield Turnpike Trust with a toll-house at Shenstone Woodend.

Collett Brook Toll-house, Bassetts Pole
SP 144989
Roads into Tamworth

photo: tim jenkinson

FOX HILL RD.

Roads radiating from the town of Tamworth, first turnpiked in 1770, included a section from Bourne Bridge to Bassett's Pole on the Warwickshire border, where this brick built two storey toll-house remains very close to the highway. It is at the junction of Fox Hill Road with what is now the A453, about two miles north-east of Sutton Coldfield towards Tamworth.

Grade II listed, it retains its octagonal end, porch and space for a toll-board to the left of the window above the doorway on the east side. This side view of the property from 2011 shows how dilapidated the house had become with its windows boarded up, however it is now undergoing repair. The toll-house doubled as a farm and was used to collect tolls for the Tamworth Turnpike Trust in the 19th Century.

Weeford Toll-house
(SK 133047)   'T.G.'
Lichfield - Stone etc.

Built on a section of Watling Street between the towns of Tamworth and Brownhills that runs parallel with the new A5, a toll-house once operated as 'Weeford Gate' just north of the village at the junction with the present day A38.

It appeared as 'T.G.' on early 19th Century OS maps, but by the time of the 1871 Census the house had stopped being used for collecting tolls and was occupied by 55 year old 'Agricultural labourer' Charles Passam, his wife Mary and their two teenage sons Thomas and William.

Four Lost Tamworth Toll-houses

Roads into Tamworth

Comberford Toll-house,
(SK 195072) 'T.G.' **Wiggington**
Roads into Tamworth

This Tamworth Trust toll-house was built on the turnpike road towards Rugeley about two miles north of the town on what is the present day A513. It stood at or near the junction of the lane to Comberford and appears as a 'T.G.' on early 19th Century OS maps.

In the Census of 1871 the toll-house is recorded as the 'Comberford Gate' with 42 year old 'toll contractor' Thomas Lees, his 'toll-collector' wife Hannah and their five children in residence.

Glascote Road Toll-house,
(SK 215036) 'T.G.' **Tamworth**
Roads into Tamworth

Positioned in Glascote Road on the present day B5000, this toll-house, a little more than half a mile from Tamworth town centre, collected tolls from travellers coming in from the direction of Ashby de la Zouch.

Often coupled with the nearby Kettlebrook toll-house in turnpike records, it was occupied in 1871 by 28 year old 'miner' Reuben Hull, his wife Esther, the probable toll-collector, and their 4 children.

Bitterscote Toll-house, Tamworth
(SK 205036) 'T.G.'
Roads into Tamworth

Also shown as 'T.G.' on the early OS maps, this toll-house appears to have been at the junction of the present day A453 with the A4091. Due to extensive road widening and realignment at this point it is difficult to provide the exact location.

It was however, the first toll-gate along the Sutton Road out of Tamworth in what was then the hamlet of Bitterscote. The toll-house was occupied in 1861 by 'Toll-collector' Fanny Hankin, her 'Labourer at Paper Mill' husband Thomas and their four young children.

Kettlebrook Toll-house,
(SK 214034) 'T.G.' **Tamworth**
Roads into Tamworth

Again marked 'T.G.' on early 19th Century OS maps, it seems that a toll-house once stood in the vicinity of the old Lamb Inn in Kettlebrook Road, now the site of the entrance to the Tamworth Football Club's ground.

The toll-house is recorded under the name of 'Kettlebrook' in the Parish of Bolehall and Glascote in the 1871 Census with 'labourer' Edwin Wilkinson and his wife Mary living there, whereas ten years earlier 'toll-collector' Samuel Allen and his family were in residence.

Packington Lane Toll-house, Hopwas
SK 170050 'T.G.'
Roads into Tamworth

photo: tim jenkinson

Standing on the corner of Packington Lane this curiously extended house, now known as 'Tollgate Cottage', is in the position of a 'T.G.' shown on early 19th Century OS maps. It stands a quarter mile from the village of Hopwas on the A51, originally the Tamworth to Lichfield turnpike.

The original house seems to have been incorporated into a much larger building but nonetheless retains a curious low slit window on the side wall facing into the lane as well as a bay window possibly where the porch once stood.

Bourne Brook Toll-house,
(SK 172013) 'T.G.' **Drayton Bassett**
Roads into Tamworth

Built on the road towards Sutton Coldfield by the Tamworth Turnpike Trust this toll-house stood at the junction of the lane leading to Hill Farm.

It was recorded in the Census returns of 1871 in the Parish of Drayton Bassett with at that time 43 year old Fanny Hewkin working as the 'toll-collector' and living there with her husband Thomas and their three young children.

Recorded as the 'Hopwas Toll-Gate, Weeford, Swinfen and Packington' in the Census of 1861 it was occupied at that time by 46 year old 'Jobbing shepherd and toll-collector' Edward Smith, his wife Ann and their 17 year old niece Emma.

Fazeley Junction Toll-house
SK 203020
Birmingham & Fazeley Canal

photo: tim jenkinson

This large and impressive two storey toll-house stands at the junction of the Birmingham and Fazeley Canal with the Coventry Canal. From here the latter continues to the north-east passing through Tamworth, Atherstone, Nuneaton and Bedworth and then on to Coventry, a distance of some 27 miles. The Birmingham and Fazeley Canal, completed in 1789, continues to the south and eventually meets the Trent and Mersey Canal eleven miles away at Fradley Junction.

Coleshill Road Toll-house,
(SK 199010) 'T.G.' **Drayton Bassett**
Roads into Tamworth

Marked as a 'T.G.' on early OS maps this toll-house stood a little way north of Drayton Lane on what is now the A4091, that once formed part of the Tamworth to Coleshill Turnpike from 1770.

The house was occupied in 1871 by 42 year old 'toll-collector' Elizabeth Wright her husband James and their two children Agnes and Henry.

Dating from the mid 19th Century the Fazeley toll-house retains its tall octagonal end facing the canal, and has quite large wings to both sides. The building was grade II listed in 1987 as the 'Junction House' along with the nearby Tow Path (Roving) Bridge. Abandoned and boarded up in 2007, the toll-house has since reverted to a private dwelling.

Watling Street Toll-house, Wilnecote
(SK 215016)
Roads into Tamworth

photo: tamworth castle

This large two storey traditionally styled toll-house once stood at the foot of Quarry Hill at its junction with Watling Street, west of the village of Wilnecote. About two miles south of Tamworth, the crossroads here formed by the A5 and A51 is still known as 'Two Gates'.

As can be seen from this old photograph dating from c.1906, the house once had a blanked window above the door where a toll-board would have been fixed. In 1861 it appears as 'Toll Bar Watling Street Road' with 26 year old 'Toll-collector' Ann Sea, her 'coal miner' husband Henry and their three children in residence.

Kingsbury Lane Toll-house
(SP 217958) 'T.G.' **(Warwicks)**
Roads into Tamworth

A 'T.G.' is shown on early OS maps south of the village of Kingsbury near what was Kingsbury Mill on the Tamworth to Nuneaton turnpike (A51) at the junction with what is now an old disused road to Curdworth opposite Mill Crescent.

The toll-house appears as the 'Kingsbury Lane Toll-gate' in the Census returns of 1861, occupied at that time by 59 year old 'toll-collector' Elizabeth Taylor and her 'platelayer' husband Thomas.

The rapid speed of change along this road in the 20th Century necessitated the toll-house's demolition at some point, most probably for road widening.

More Lost Tamworth Toll-houses

Rugeley - Alrewas

Loopin Lane Toll-house,
(SK 147158)   **King's Bromley**
Rugeley - Alrewas

Towards the end of the road from Rugeley to Alrewas, there was a toll-house just past Kings Bromley, appearing under the name of 'Loopin Lane' in 1851 with 67 year old 'Chelsea Pensioner' George Hitchin and his wife Mary there.
It was probably where the lane, (now Lupin), joins the A513 at Orgreave, however early OS maps show a 'T.G.' about a mile further east nearer Alrewas at SK 161153. By 1871 it was occupied by 'Cordwainer and Toll-gate keeper' William B. Jinks his wife Elizabeth and six children.

Elford Toll-house
(SK 192100)
Roads into Tamworth

Recorded in the Census returns of 1871 somewhere between the old Mill and the village of Elford on the main Tamworth to King's Bromley turnpike, present day A513, this toll-house probably stood just south of the point where the road into the village forks away from the main highway.

No longer in evidence the house was occupied at that time by 46 year old 'Toll-collector' Mary Lees, probably a relative of the toll-collecting occupants of the nearby Comberford Gate (p.70).

Roads into Tamworth

Oakley Toll-house, Croxall
(SK 192139)   'T.G.'
Roads into Tamworth

Marked as a 'T.G.' on early 19th Century maps and dating from c.1826, this toll-house became known as 'Oakley Gate'. Built close to the main Tamworth to Kings Bromley turnpike (A513) half a mile west of the village of Croxall, it also controlled roads to Walton on Trent and Edindale.

In 1871 the 'toll-gate keeper' was Oxfordshire born 26 year old Charles Beesley living there with his wife Mary Ann and their two young children.

Main Road Toll-house, Harlaston
(SK 216111)
Roads into Tamworth

A toll-gate and house once operated in the village of Harlaston close to the Staffordshire-Derbyshire border. Although the location is uncertain Census returns place the house on what is now Main Road running through the village, not far from the White Lion Inn. A section of road leading from Elford Mill through Harlaston to Clifton Campville was turnpiked under an Act of 1770.

Occupied in 1871 by the Wright family when giving its name to a number of dwellings in the area, it is 31 year old Elizabeth Wright who is recorded as the 'toll-gate keeper', living there with husband William and their six children all under 10 years old.

High Bridge Toll-house, Mavesyn Ridware
SK 091170   'T.G.'
High Bridge - Uttoxeter etc.

photo: tim jenkinson

An Act of 1766 permitted a turnpike from High Bridge near Armitage northwards through Hill Ridware and Abbots Bromley on to Uttoxeter. Appearing under the name of 'High Bridge' in the Census returns of 1841, this now large and rather imposing two storey square ended toll-house stands half a mile to the east of the village of Mavesyn Ridware on what is now the B5014.

It has a recessed panel on the side facing into the road where a toll-board was most likely affixed. By 1861 it is recorded simply as the 'Toll-Gate House' with 'Toll-gate keeper' Benjamin Brough, his wife Sarah and their two sons in residence. Today the house retains the name but has become a small garden centre.

Armitage Toll-house
(SK 082161)
Rugeley - Alrewas

The road from Rugeley through Armitage to Handsacre (A513) was turnpiked under an Act of 1824. Built near enough in the fork of Old and New Roads in the village of Armitage a toll-house operated at a point that was to become known as 'Gate Square'.

It is recorded in the Census of 1871 between the Swan 'Beerhouse' and the then 'Wilson's Cottages' on the site where there is now a shop. At that time it was occupied by 'Toll-collector' Mary Morris and 14 year old 'domestic servant' Anne Holmes.

Lost Burton Upon Trent Toll-houses

Ryknild Street

Stretton Moor Toll-house
(SK 255254)   'T.G.'
Burton upon Trent - Derby

Marked as a 'T.G.' on early 19th Century OS maps a toll-house was built at Stretton Moor on the present day A5121 (Ryknild Street) close to the then turn to Wetmoor Hall on the Burton to Derby road, turnpiked in 1753.
The toll-house is recorded in the Census of 1841 as the 'Stretton Toll-Gate' with 70 year old 'Toll-gate keeper' Thomas Walker in residence.

Branston Toll-house
(SK 222211)   'T.G.'
Lichfield - Stone etc.

The Burton to Lichfield road was turnpiked in 1729 and some thirty years later a toll-house and gate had been built in the village of Branston. Old maps show a 'T.G.' at the junction of present day Main Street with   what was Tatenhill Lane, leading north to Rough Hay over Branston Bridge.
The toll-house was occupied in 1871 by Leicestershire born 'toll-collector' Mary Tipler, her 'agricultural labourer' husband Jabez, their son Edmund and granddaughter Ann Murphy. The name of the 'Gate' lives on in a nearby hostelry, the road through Branston having been by-passed in the late 1980's with the construction of the new Lichfield Road.

Ashby - Tutbury

Horninglow Toll-house
(SK 241252)
Ashby-de-la-Zouch - Tutbury

This toll-house was situated on the east side of the village of Horninglow at the junction with Rolleston Road from around 1753. In 1852 another toll-gate was set up near the canal to the south but was taken down soon thereafter. The original toll-house appears on early 19th Century maps as 'Horninglow Gate' and by 1871 was occupied by the toll-collecting team of Thomas and Mary Appleton living there with their daughter Elizabeth.

Bearwood Hill Toll-house,
(SK 259232)   'T.G.'   **Winshill**
Ashby-de-la-Zouch - Tutbury

The road from Tutbury to Ashby-de-la-Zouch in Leicestershire was turnpiked in 1753, originally taking the line of Bearwood Hill Road and High Bank Road in Winshill. A toll-house was built near the foot of Bearwood Hill Road, just north of the present day A511, and is recorded by this name in the 1871 Census, with Sarah Showell acting as the 'toll-collector' there along with her husband Edward and their four children.
In the 1830's the Ashby Road was laid out more directly and another toll-gate was positioned near Moat Bank. Appearing as the Winshill Wood Gate and marked as a 'T.P.' on mid 19th Century OS maps, the associated toll-house at SK 273227 survived until its demolition in the 1930's.

Elms Road Toll-house, Stapenhill
SK 256227   'T.G.'
Burton upon Trent - Nuneaton

photo: tim jenkinson

The Stanton Road was turnpiked in the 18th Century, as part of the route from Measham, and by 1825 a toll-gate was operating north of the church in Stapenhill. It was later moved to the junction of Elms Road on what is now the A444 and appears at this point as 'T.G.' on early 19th Century OS maps.

In 1851 the toll-house was occupied by 32 year old 'toll-gate keeper' Joseph Rowland, his wife Sarah and several family members. Whilst it cannot be confirmed, this two storey lodge house is certainly in the right position and it may be that the part of the building closest to the Elms Road junction was used to collect tolls. There is evidence of a probable blocked doorway to the right along with a curious low window in the wall facing into the road, however, its proximity to the nearby cemetery may complicate this perception.

Walton on Trent Toll-house
(approx SK 202183)
Lichfield - Stone etc.

The location of this toll-house is uncertain but it is recorded in the Census returns of 1871 simply as 'Toll-gate Walton on Trent' with 56 year old 'agricultural labourer' Abraham Earp, his wife Ann, son and grandson in residence.
It most likely stood west of the village at a point then known as 'Barton Turning', where the road leading to Barton-Under-Needwood crossed Ryknild Street, the main Burton to Lichfield turnpike from 1729, a section now by-passed by the modern A38 trunk road.

Lost Toll-houses west of Burton Upon Trent

Ashbourne - Sudbury etc.

Aston Bridge Toll-house, Sudbury
(SK 163308)   'T.P.'
Ashbourne - Sudbury etc.

The road from Ashbourne to Yoxall Bridge
via Sudbury and Draycott in the Clay was
first turnpiked in 1766.   Just into
Staffordshire, a toll-house operated south
of Aston Bridge, just north of the present
level crossing. The coming of the railway
in the mid 19th Century probably saw the
end of the toll-house as a collecting point:
it is shown on some early OS maps but
cannot be found in Census returns.

Lichfield Rd Toll-house, Draycott
(SK 159295)   'T.G.'
Ashbourne - Sudbury etc.

An Act of Parliament in 1809 sanctioned a
new road westward from Draycott in the
Clay to Marchington and Uttoxeter, an
extension of the earlier Ashbourne to
Yoxall Bridge road. A toll-house was built
in Lichfield Road (now Main Road) at its
junction with the new road to Marchington,
which was occupied in 1871 by 58 year
old 'Toll-gate keeper' Sarah Brough and
17 year old 'lodger' William Brown.

Trent Bridge Toll-house, Yoxall
(SK 131178)   'T.G.'
Ashbourne - Sudbury etc.

At the southern end of the route south
from Ashbourne, there was a toll-house
half a mile south of Yoxall where the Trent
is crossed by Yoxall Bridge.   It was
recorded as 'Trent Bridge' in the Census
of 1861 with 53 year old 'toll-collector' Ann
Preston, her 'ag. lab.' husband Samuel,
son and grandson living there.

Burton - Shirleywich

Rough Hay Toll-house
(SK 238231)   'T.G.'
Burton - Shirleywich

A toll-house stood on what is
now the B5017 about half a
mile from Burton town centre
on the road to Abbots
Bromley, built in 1809.
Dating from c.1845 the toll-
house soon became known as
the Rough Hay toll-gate, as
recorded in the Census
returns of 1871, when 30 year
old Eliza Roe was acting as
the 'toll-collector', living there
with her husband Charles and
their two young children Sarah
and Arthur. Two years later
the roads in and around
Burton were disturnpiked.

Bromley Wood Toll-house
(SK 100242)   'T.G.'
Burton - Shirleywich

According to Phillips and
Turton (1988) an Act of 1809
sanctioned the building of a
turnpike from Burton Upon
Trent to Abbots Bromley and
from there through the village
of Newton to Shirleywich to
join the Lichfield to Stone
turnpike.
A toll-house was built on the
present day B5234 a mile or
so east of Abbots Bromley in
the fork of two roads, and was
occupied in 1861 by lone 'Toll-
gate keeper' 56 year old
Charlotte Perceval.

Great Haywood Toll-house, Colwich
SK 001234　　　'T.G.'
Lichfield - Stone etc.

photo: tim jenkinson

This now much extended toll-house, hardly recognisable as such, stands at the junction of Tolldish Lane with what is now the A51 opposite the turn to the village of Great Haywood in the parish of Colwich.

It would have operated on what was part of the Lichfield to Stone turnpike sanctioned under an Act of 1729 and is still known as the 'Old Toll-house', although the original structure would have been a simple two storey building, probably with a porch edging into the lane. It was purpose built to replace an older site (T.G.) to the south at SJ 999231 and is recorded in the Census of 1871 as the 'Haywood Toll-Gate House' with 67 year old 'Toll-gate keeper' Mary Riley in residence, living there with her 'cordwainer' son Joseph.

Wolseley Toll-house, Colwich
(SK 031199)　　　'T.G.'
Lichfield - Stone etc.

Another toll-gate operated on the main road between Lichfield and Stone on what is today the A51 about a mile from Rugeley in the parish of Wolseley.

The toll-house appears as a 'T.G.' on early 19th Century OS maps and is recorded as the 'Toll-gate house' in the district of Etchinghill in the Census returns of 1871, when it was occupied by the husband and wife toll collecting team of Edwin and Sarah Potts, living there with their one year old son William.

Chartley Toll-house, Stowe
SK 004280   'T.G.'
Roads into Stafford

photo: tim jenkinson

A much extended brick built two storey square toll-house stands in the fork of Station Road and the A518 north of Stowe-by-Chartley on the road between Stafford and Uttoxeter, turnpiked in 1793.

Now 'Tollgate Cottage', it was built by the Stafford Turnpike Trust in the early 19th Century. Curiously although grade II listed in the 1970's, it was later delisted and has thus now been greatly modified to the rear with a much larger extension.

The house appears as 'Amerton Toll-gate' in the Census of 1841 with 58 year old William Bennett as 'toll-gate keeper' and later in 1861 it appears as 'Toll-Gate House Mount Pleasant' with 22 year old 'brickmaker' Joseph Dix his wife, son and niece in residence.

Bridge Toll-house, Sandon
(SJ 946289)
Stafford - Sandon etc.

An early 15th Century bridge with two stone arches and refuges for pedestrians carries the present day B5066 from Sandonbank to Little Sandon.

Around 400 years later a toll-house operated on the bridge appearing under the name 'Sandon Gate' in the Census returns of 1851, with 88 year old 'toll-gate keeper' Hannah Anderson living there with James and Hannah Perkin and four year old Mariann Betterley.

By 1861 the occupants of the 'Sandon Bridge Toll-gate' had become 38 year old widow and 'toll-gate keeper' Elizabeth Kinsey, her son and two daughters.

Weston Toll-house
(SJ 972271)
Roads into Stafford

A toll-house in the village of Weston -upon-Trent operated close to the Saracen's Head public house on the south side of the road and is recorded as such in the Census of 1871, occupied at that time by 22 year old dressmaker Hannah Riley and her two sisters who may have been doubling as the 'toll-collector'.

The two storey house with central chimney was one of two buildings on what is now the A518 that were known collectively as the 'toll-houses' surviving until demolition in c.1970's when the present day 'Four Winds' was constructed. This needlework pattern by Mrs Ruth Allen reproduced from an old photograph shows the position of the two houses and their proximity to the road.

Hopton Toll-house
(SJ 942270 approx)
Stafford - Sandon etc.

The road between Stafford and Sandon was first turnpiked in 1763 to link the town with the then Lichfield to Stone road. Although the location of the Hopton toll-house is uncertain it may have been built at the junction of either Within or Hopton Lane with what is today the B5066.

It is recorded as the 'Hopton Toll Bar' in 1861, with 64 year old 'toll-collector' John Glover and his 'assistant toll-collector' wife Margaret and 10 year old nephew John Taylor at the house. The name of 'Tollgate' lives on in the 21st Century in a nearby industrial estate.

Four Lost Toll-houses South of Stafford

Roads into Stafford

Stone - Wordsley Green

Castle Gate Toll-house, Castle
(SJ 904220)   **Church**
Roads into Stafford

This toll-house was built near enough outside the entrance to Stafford Castle on the Newport Road. It appears in successive Census returns of the mid to late 19th Century as the 'Castle Toll-Bar' and was occupied in 1871 by 27 year old 'Shoemaker' William Hodgson his wife Martha, their two sons and daughter.

Billington Toll-house, Castle
(SJ 894213)   'T.G.'   **Church**
Roads into Stafford

Built not far from the Castle Gate on the road towards Newport (A518), this toll-house stood at the junction with a road leading north to the village of Derrington.

It appeared in the Census returns of 1871 as the 'Billington Toll Gate' with 55 year old 'Shoemaker' Thomas Moore living at the house with his wife Ann. It seems that both he and nearby 'shoemaker' William Hodgson were doubling as toll-collectors at that time.

This may well be the toll-house that is described by Robert Sherlock (1976) at 'Thorneyfields' a small single storey cottage with gable end and space below to support a toll-board. It is unclear as to when or why the building was demolished.

Rowley Bank Toll-house,
(SJ 921221)   **Stafford**
Stone - Wordsley Green etc.

A toll-gate, probably with a toll-house, was once positioned at the foot of Rowley Bank on the road leading to Wolverhampton at the entrance to Rowley Park in Stafford.

This must have been a source of great annoyance to travellers moving between the two towns who would also encounter gates at nearby Rising Brook (the Hyde Lea Gate) and at Acton (Catch Corner).

Hyde Lea Toll-house, Rising
(SJ 920214)   **Brook**
Stone - Wordsley Green etc.

This toll-house was built c.1831 by the Stafford Trust about a mile from the town centre in Rising Brook on part of what was the Stone to Wordsley Green turnpike of 1761 (1 GIII c.39) that passed through Wolverhampton along the present day A449.

It was positioned near the junction of the unclassified Coppenhall Road leading southwards to Hyde Lea and subsequently became known by that name in the turnpike reports and records of the time.

Shirleywich Toll-house, Weston
SJ 984259
Lichfield - Stone etc.

photo: tim jenkinson

A Turnpike Act of 1809 sanctioned the building of a road from Burton upon Trent passing through Abbots Bromley and Newton to Shirleywich in Weston, on the Lichfield to Stone road.

Donald Massey (2002) states that the former Ferrers Arms and toll-house at Shirleywich are still in evidence as a private dwelling, between the London to Chester Road and the canal.

The large building at this point, a little north-west of Amerton Lane, seems part of a farmhouse but possesses on the north-east side facing the road (A51) a large projecting porch with a low window on either side, the only evidence that might confirm its former role. The house underwent considerable renovation in 2011/12.

Cannock Road Toll-house,
(SJ 951201) 'T.G.' **Brocton**
Roads into Stafford

A 'T.G.' is shown near the junction of Acton Hill with the Cannock Road in Brocton on the present day A34 about two miles south-east of Stafford town.

A lone white house 'Swansford' stands on the corner of the road leading south to Acton Trussell here, but it is set back from the road and its role seems unlikely and cannot be confirmed.

Four Lost Toll-houses North of Stafford

Stafford - Sandon etc.

Great Bridgeford Toll-house
(SJ 884269)
Stafford - Sandon etc.

David Vincent (1982) explains that tolls were collected on the Stafford - Sandon - Eccleshall Turnpike from 1763 and a gate or house operated in the village of Great Bridgeford on what is the present day A5013 probably near where the B5405 from Woodseaves joins the main road.

This toll-gate along with another in Eccleshall outside the then Royal Oak controlled that section of road into the village that went on to Woore in Cheshire via gates at Sugnall, Bearstone and Dorrington.

Gnosall Toll-house
(SJ 827205)
Roads into Stafford

Appearing under the registration district of Newport in 1871 and therefore at the time in the county of Shropshire, the toll-bar at Gnosall was positioned at the junction of Wharf Road (Moreton Road) and the A518 Stafford to Newport road, at the site of present day Oak Cottage.

The Census of that year records 51 year old 'Agricultural labourer' Samuel Belfield, his wife Ann and their five children at the house.

Stone - Wordsley Green

Yarlet Hill Toll-house, Whitgreave
(SJ 908277)   'T.G.'
Stone - Wordsley Green etc.

This toll-house was built by the Stone, Stafford and Penkridge Turnpike Trust on the present day A34 on Yarlet Hill at the point where Whitgreave Lane joins the main road about three miles north of Stafford town on what was part of the original 1761 turnpike between Stone and Wordsley Green in Kingswinford.

Marked as a 'T.G.' on early OS maps, the toll-house was occupied in 1861 by 'Carpenter and Toll-gate keeper' John Smith and his family. Both his wife Catherine and their 12 year old son Albert are also listed as 'toll-gate keepers'.

Tillington Toll-house
(SJ 911247)   'T.G.'
Stafford - Sandon etc.

Another toll-gate was positioned in that area of Stafford known as Tillington near the junction of the A5013 road to Eccleshall with present day Holmcroft Road, the latter not in evidence at the time of the early 19th Century.
This was part of the Stafford to Sandon turnpike of 1763 branching through Great Bridgeford into Eccleshall. A toll-house was subsequently built at the site and in both 1861 and 1871 the occupier is recorded as John Palmer 'renter of turnpike tolls', living there with his wife Maria.

Canal Toll-house, Great Haywood
SJ 994229
Staffs & Worcs Canal

photo: tim jenkinson

This small brick built single storey toll-house with chimney can still be seen beside the tow path on a section of the Staffordshire and Worcestershire Canal close to the point where it joins the Trent and Mersey Canal, near the village of Great Haywood.

The toll-house retains three interesting round arched windows two on the side walls and one on the front beside the door all of which are currently protected by a wire mesh. In recent times the former toll-house has been used as a small craft shop.

Weeping Cross Toll-house, Baswich
(SJ 944214)
Roads into Stafford

A relatively late addition to the toll-houses of the Stafford Turnpike Trust, records show that by 1834 a house was being used for collecting tolls at Weeping Cross in Baswich.

It was built to replace a much earlier gate at Forebridge nearer the town, and was most likely positioned at the fork of the two roads that divide east to Lichfield (A513) and south to Cannock (A34).

The toll-house was also well positioned for catching travellers moving along Baswich Lane and was probably demolished as part of necessary road widening at what has now become a busy intersection of roads.

Four Lost Eccleshall Toll-houses

Eccleshall - Newcastle under Lyme

Sugnall Toll-house, Croxton
(SJ 793317)   'T.G.'
Stafford - Sandon etc.

This toll-house was built on a branch of the Stafford to Sandon, Eccleshall and District Turnpike near the village of Croxton on what is now the B5026.
It became known as the 'Sugnall Toll-gate' and appears under this name in the Census returns of the mid 19th Century. In 1861 the toll-house was occupied by 83 year old 'Toll-gate keeper' Enoch Shaw, his wife Jane and their two year old grandson Edwin Brock.   David Vincent (1982) refers to this house as the 'Westland Gate'.

Castle Street Toll-house
(SJ 831295)   'T.G.'
Eccleshall - Newcastle under Lyme

In 1823 the road between Newcastle and Eccleshall was rebuilt and tolls were collected not far out of the latter, outside the entrance to the castle on what is the present day A519.
According to Vincent (1982) this particular collection point was a source of great annoyance to the then Bishop of Eccleshall James Cornwallis who campaigned unsuccessfully to have it removed.

In 1861 it is recorded as the 'Castle Street Toll-house', occupied by 'Toll-gate keeper and domestic gardener' Thomas Bagworth and his wife Ann.

Slindon Toll-house
(SJ 825332)
Eccleshall - Newcastle under Lyme

This toll-house is recorded in the Census returns of 1871 with 36 year old 'agricultural labourer' Alfred Rushton acting as the 'toll-collector', living there with his wife Martha and their five young children. It stood on what is now the A519 Eccleshall to Newcastle-Under-Lyme road probably where it bends eastward towards Mill Meece.

The likeliest site is on the corner of a minor road leading north to Standon approximately a mile from Slindon village. This would have effectively covered the route leading south from the present day A51 on the Stone to Nantwich turnpike, and would have cut off those attempting to evade the tolls at Stableford by taking minor routes.

Hilcott Toll-house, Chebsey
(SJ 846296)
Stone - Longton etc.

A third toll-house operated on the Stone to Eccleshall road (B5026) at approximately one mile east of the latter at the turn to Hilcott Hall on a cross-roads to the north west of the village of Chebsey.

Recorded as the 'Hilcott Toll-bar' in the Census of 1861 the 'collector of tolls' at that time was 72 year old Daniel Thomas.

Littleworth Toll-house, Stafford
(SJ 932233)   'T.G.'
Roads into Stafford

photo: staffordshire arts and museum service

This two storey toll-house was built in the fork of two roads, one to Weston the other to Tixall, in Littleworth about half a mile from Stafford, when these roads were first turnpiked in 1793 as part of all routes radiating from the town. The old photo above is dated c.1870 and clearly shows how both roads here were gated. A toll board is visible above the doorway.

Demolished c.1878 upon the demise of the Turnpike Trust the house was later replaced by a public house that until recently retained the name of 'The Gate' but is now 'The Metropolitan Bar'. Marked as a 'T.G.' on early OS maps, the toll-taker in the photograph is probably 40 year old Susannah Grimes who is recorded at the house in the Census returns of 1871, living there with her three children.

Catch Corner Toll-house, Acton
(SJ 928193)   'T.G.'   **Trussell** *Stone - Wordsley Green etc.*

Now the site of a busy roundabout this toll-house marked as a 'T.G.' on early OS maps of the 19th Century, was built near the turn to the village of Acton Trussell on the Wolverhampton Road now classified as the A4449.

The toll-house appears simply as 'Toll-bar' in the Census of 1871 with 37 year old 'shoemaker' Edmund Lake his wife and son in residence. Both the name of Catch Corner and Acton Gate live on in the names of nearby buildings at a point where motorists join the M6 at junction 13 just south of here.

Four Lost Stone Toll-houses

Lichfield - Stone etc.

Stone Field Toll-house, Meaford
(SJ 893346)   'T.G.'
Lichfield - Stone etc.

Clearly shown as a toll-gate on early 19th Century OS maps, this toll-house once stood near the point where the Newcastle road out from the town meets the present day A34 dual carriageway Stone by-pass, roughly at the turn off the roundabout.
It was occupied in 1851 by 53 year old 'Toll-gate keeper' Mary Merrick, her daughter and lodger Thomas Emery.   Given its obvious precarious position at this point it was most probably a victim of road widening in the 20th Century.

Scamnell Toll-house, Chebsey
(SJ 864302)
Stone - Longton etc.

This toll-house appears as the 'Scamnell Gate' in the Census returns of 1861 with 40 year old Richard Taverner recorded as 'Cordwainer and Toll-Gate Keeper' living there with his family.
It was built two miles to the east of Eccleshall on what is now the B5026, at a point where Scamnell Lane branches off south to Chebsey village. It was the second of three such gates operating on this road between Stone and Eccleshall and today there is an interesting two storey building at the site, but it is dated 1887, just after the turnpike era had ended.

Stone - Longton etc.

Longton Road Toll-house, Stone
(SJ 901343)   'T.G.'
Stone - Longton etc.

Shown as 'T.G.' on early OS maps this toll-gate stood close to the town centre of Stone at the start of Longton Road, near Radford Street where the road to Oulton goes north.

Probably dating from the time of the turnpike in 1771, the toll-house was occupied in 1861 by 46 year old 'toll-collector and labourer' James Winfield, his wife Elizabeth and their five children. Although an earlier toll-gate it would have worked at this time in conjunction with the Hayes Bank toll-house a mile further out.

Micklow Toll-house, Walton
(SJ 885324)   'T.G.'
Stone - Longton etc.

From 1792 the first toll-gate on the road out of Stone towards Eccleshall stood at Micklow in Walton and is marked as a 'T.G.' on early OS maps. It stood near where the road now crosses over the M6 motorway.
In 1851 the toll-house was recorded as 'uninhabited at night' but ten years later the 'Micklow Toll Gate' was occupied by 31 year old 'Cordwainer' Henry Taverner, his wife Susannah and their 10 year old son Henry junior, probably relatives of the inhabitants of the nearby Scamnell Gate. It is most probably the toll-house referred to as 'Cold Norton' by David Vincent (1982).

Whitley Heath Toll-house, Eccleshall
SJ 816259
Ellenhall - Newport

photo: tim jenkinson

This low single storey brick built cottage once operated as a toll-gate on the Eccleshall to Newport road in the hamlet of Whitley Heath on what is now the A519 a little way west of where Cash Lane joins the main route close to a sharp bend.

Now known as the 'Old Tollgate Cottage', the original house has been extended to the side and rear but retains its doorway facing into the road. The toll-board may have been affixed in the space to the side of the right hand window

33 year old 'cordwainer and toll-collector' William Owen is recorded at the house in 1851, living there with his wife Anne and their two sons John and Charles. This is likely to be the toll-gate at Woodseaves referred to by David Vincent in 1982.

Forton Toll-house
(SJ 753212)
Ellenhall - Newport

Tolls were collected in the village of Forton on what was the Eccleshall to Newport road, the present day A519, which was turnpiked as part of an Act of 1804 (44 GIII c.25).

It worked in conjunction with the Whitley Heath toll-house on the road into Shropshire a mere two miles from Newport. It was most likely built at or near the junction with a minor road leading north to the village of Adbaston and may be the Flint's Gate that is referred to in various Turnpike records.

Hayes Bank Toll-house, Oulton
(SJ 914353)
Stone - Longton etc.

photo: valerie bell

The original road from Stone to Longton was turnpiked in 1771 (11 GIII c.86) and this toll-house at Hayes Bank became one of two gates operating near to the town. Built at the foot of Rockwoods opposite the then flint mill at Hayes, the small single storey cottage marshalled passage into the town just to the north-east of Oulton Cross where present day Nicholl's Lane and The Hays join the main A520.

Small as it seems, it was occupied in 1861 by 46 year old 'Toll-collector and labourer' James Winfield, his wife Elizabeth and their five children with 25 year old daughter Mary recorded as an 'Assistant Collector of Tolls'. Still in evidence in the 1920's the house later became an unfortunate victim of road widening at this point.

Hollywood Toll-house, Sandon
(SJ 935332)   'T.G.'
Uttoxeter - Stone etc.

Another toll-gate operated on the road between Little Stoke and Milwich from around 1793 on what is the present day B5027 at Hollywood. The toll-house, marked as a 'T.G.' on early OS maps, stood a little way to the west of the junction of a minor road leading down from the hamlet of Cotwalton.

The building may have been abandoned as a turnpike house by the mid 19th Century as it seems to be not recorded in the Census returns of that time.

London Road Toll-house, Salt
SJ 968279   'T.P.'
Derby - Newcastle under Lyme

photo: tim jenkinson

Often referred to as 'toll-house farm', this large isolated building with a generous plot of land and out-house still stands on the south side of the busy dual carriageway London to Chester road (A51), between the villages of Sandon and Weston. Set a short way back from the road edge it has a most unusual tall projecting gable bearing the date 1905, probably indicative of some kind of post-turnpike era alteration or possible rebuild at the site.

The toll-house would have caught travellers attempting to evade tolls by joining the main road by passing through the nearby village of Salt. On the market for £170,000 in July 2014, according to the estate agent it has leaded windows to the front and side and rather basic amenities requiring considerable modernisation and refurbishment.

Hilderstone Toll-house
(SJ 950348)   'T.G.'
Sandon - Bullock Smithy

A toll-gate is shown on early 19th Century OS maps in the heart of the village of Hilderstone, close to the Sandon to Meir Heath road (B5066). The toll-house seems to have been built a short way along present day Creswell Road that branches off north-eastwards by the church.

It appears in the 1841 Census returns as 'Toll Gate Hilderstone' occupied by 25 year old 'shoemaker' Richard Plant, his wife Elizabeth and their two young children, but its use may have subsequently been discontinued, as it does not appear in later records.

Uttoxeter Road Toll-house, Milwich
SJ 971323
Uttoxeter - Stone etc.

photo: tim jenkinson

The road between Stone and Uttoxeter was turnpiked in 1793 and this grade II listed toll-house in the village of Milwich may well date from around that time. The two storey building standing opposite the Green Man public house still retains its angled front but has been considerably extended to the side and rear. The toll-gates have been incorporated into the garden fencing either side of the house.

Long standing 'toll-keeper' Elizabeth Gratwich is recorded at the house in both the Censuses of 1851 and 1861, the latter with her 16 year old daughter Margaret. Tolls gathered from gates along this road amassed over £216 in 1848 but were eventually abolished in the late 1870's. Today it is still known as the 'Round House'.

Bramshall Toll-house
(SK 075339)   'T.G.'
Uttoxeter - Stone etc.

The road between Uttoxeter and Stone was turnpiked in 1793. Marked as a 'T.G.' on early 19th Century OS maps a toll-house was built approximately one mile west of Uttoxeter on present day B5027.

It stood close to the junction of a minor road leading back into the town and became known as the Bramshall Toll-gate due to its proximity to that village, it appears under this name in the 1871 Census returns with 'toll-collector' William Clarke and his family in residence.

Balance Hill Toll-house, Uttoxeter
(SJ 088330) 'T.G.'
High Bridge - Uttoxeter etc.

photo: staffordshire arts and museum service

Staffordshire Past Track identify this two storey brick building as a toll-house, but place it at Blounts Green, where the Stafford to Uttoxeter turnpike (A518) joined the High Bridge to Uttoxeter route (B5013). However early OS maps show a 'T.G.' further east at the foot of Balance Hill. The old photo above dates from c.1924 and shows the house to be of similar construction to others in the area such as the surviving house at Alton with a doorway to the road edge flanked by two ground floor windows.

The house appears under the name of 'Balance Hill Tollgate' in successive Census returns of the mid 19th Century and in 1871 was occupied by 46 year old 'Toll-gate keeper' Hannah Tooth living there with her three daughters. It was probably demolished during road widening sometime in the 1950's.

Cuckolds Haven Toll-house,
(SK 073297) 'T.G.' **Kingstone**
High Bridge - Uttoxeter etc.

Situated about 3 miles south-west of Uttoxeter, on what is the present day B5013 in the Parish of Kingstone, the 'Cuckolds Haven' gate is recorded in the Census returns of 1871 with lone 'toll-collector' 75 year old Ellen Riley at the toll-house.

Shown as 'T.G.' on early OS maps it seems to have been positioned just south of the junction with a minor road running north-west to the village of Loxley Green off what would have been the High Bridge to Uttoxeter turnpike of 1766.

Highwood Road Toll-house, Uttoxeter
SK 095326　　　'T.P.'
Ashbourne - Sudbury etc.

photo: tim jenkinson

This still extant toll-house now known as 'Toll Gate Cottage' stands in Highwood Road in the fork of what would have been an old route to Balance Hill off the present day B5017 from Draycott in the Clay. Highlighted in 1976 by Robert Sherlock, it was apparently built in 1831 to help with increasing toll collection for the ailing Uttoxeter Callingwood Plain Turnpike Trust.

The two storey brick built house seems to have been extended to the side and a large bay window has been inserted into the front wall facing into the road that may have once been a doorway and porch underneath a toll-board.

It is recorded simply as 'Tollgate' in High Wood in the 1861 Census returns.

Netherland Green Toll-house
(SK 102309)
Ashbourne - Sudbury etc.

This house is recorded in the 1871 Census returns as the 'Netherland Green Tollgate House', occupied by 'agricultural labourer and toll collector' Samuel Preston, his wife Kezia and their three sons with brother in law Joseph Oakden and his sister Jemima also in residence.

Two miles south of Uttoxeter, the toll-house probably stood in the hamlet of Netherland Green on the main road (B5017) near the junction of a minor road going west towards Kingstone and would have been part of the then Uttoxeter Callingwood Plain Trust.

Dove Bridge Toll-house, Ellastone
SK 120424   'T.G.'
Darley Moor - Ellastone etc.

photo: tim jenkinson

An Act of 1769 permitted the build of a turnpike from Darley Moor in Derbyshire over the River Dove at Ellastone through Ramshorn and Three Lows as far as Winkhill Bank on the Ashbourne to Leek road.

This two storey toll-cottage was built in Dove Street close to the Derbyshire border just north of the new Dove Bridge on what is the Staffordshire part of the present day B5033. Considerably extended to the rear and side the original building may well have had a porch jutting into the road.

Recorded simply as 'Dove Bridge, Rocester' in the Census returns of 1851 'Toll collectors' Robert and Mary Lock are living at the house at that time with their 'Boot and Shoemaker' son Thomas. By 1871 the house had become known as the 'Dove Bridge Toll -Gate, Ellastone'.

Uttoxeter Heath Toll-house
(SK 076347)   'T.G.'
Derby - Newcastle under Lyme

In 1823 an Act of Parliament was passed to allow three diversions to the main Newcastle to Derby turnpike, one of which was a branch between Checkley and Uttoxeter Heath along the present day A522.

A toll-house was built on the heath and is shown as 'T.G.' on early OS maps, about a mile north-west of the town, a short distance west of what is now the first roundabout on that route. The toll-house appears in the 1871 Census as 'Toll-gate St Mary's' occupied by 32 year old 'agricultural labourer' John Smith his wife Louisa and infant son Stephen.

Middle Mayfield Toll-house
SK 143444   'T.G.'
High Bridge - Uttoxeter etc.

photo: tim jenkinson

Robert Sherlock (1976) describes this toll-house as being built in the same style as that at High Bridge, presumably a large square two storey building. On the north side of the B5032 Uttoxeter to Hanging Bridge road, this square ended house, now greatly extended to the side fits the description and bears the name 'Toll-gate Cottage Calwych 1997', the date of recent renovation. There is evidence of a blocked doorway on the left of the wall facing into the road and a window above may have once supported a toll-board.

In 1861 the main occupant of the 'Toll-gate House, Middle Mayfield', was 56 year old 'Toll-collector' Elizabeth Salt, living there with her 'dressmaker' daughter Sarah. She appears again in the 1881 Census, possibly at the same house, but this time as 'formerly toll-collector'.

Wood Lane Toll-house,
(SK 095330)   'T.P.'   **Uttoxeter**
High Bridge - Uttoxeter etc.

In his 'Memories of Uttoxeter' account of 1880-1910, Chemist Ernest Martin Mellor recalls there being a toll-gate at the junction of Wood Lane and High Wood (now Highwood Road) to the south of the town, close to the present day racecourse.

Indeed the house is recorded in the 1861 Census simply as 'Tollgate House' and is shown as a 'T.P.' on late 19th Century OS maps of the area as near a malt house, now demolished. The toll-house on Highwood Road further south is also shown on this map.

Birdsgrove Lane Toll-house, Upper Mayfield
SK 157461
Ashbourne - Leek etc.

photo: tim jenkinson

Close to the Staffordshire-Derbyshire border in Upper Mayfield this grade II listed house, now 'Tollgate Cottage', was used to collect tolls on the Ashbourne to Leek Turnpike (present day A52) at the start of Swinscoe Hill. It stands at the junction of that road with Birdsgrove Lane that leads to the village of Okeover. The two storey house has a distinctive octagonal end facing the road where a large space above the window probably held a toll-board.

Built in 1842 for just £95 the house looks to have been considerably extended to the side but retains a number of gothick styled windows in support of its turnpike heritage. In 1871 at the time of the Census the 'Tollgate House' was occupied by 41 year old 'Ag Lab' Herbert Wheeldon and his daughters Hannah and Eliza.

Quixhill Bank Toll-house,
(SK 102414)   **Denstone**
Cheadle - Rocester etc.

A 'Gate House' is recorded in the Census returns of 1871 in the vicinity of Denstone Hall near Quixhill on what is now the B5032.

Tolls were probably being collected from a house at the junction of Quixhill Lane with the main turnpike just before it met the Spath to Hanging Bridge road to the north. An alternative site could be further south nearer Denstone where the two main roads fork.

Old Turnpike Toll-house, Stramshall
SK 067374
High Bridge - Uttoxeter etc.

Although its role in the turnpike era cannot be confirmed, this rather atypical two storey house is nevertheless in the right position on an unclassified road between Stramshall and Hollington to have been useful for collecting tolls. Retaining the name 'Turnpike Cottage' it stands on a section of road that is recorded as the 'Old Turnpike' on early 19th Century OS maps. Set a little back from the road it looks to have been extended to the side but may have once had a porch and gate to arrest travellers.

photo: tim jenkinson

From 1766 this may have been part of a main route between Uttoxeter and Rocester, probably a branch of the early Spath to Hanging Bridge turnpike that was subsequently revised and superseded by Acts of 1787, 1808 and 1828 that took the road nearer the river, further east through the hamlet of Crakemarsh and Combridge.

Crakemarsh Toll-house, Spath (SK 086352) 'T.G.' *High Bridge - Uttoxeter etc.*	**Waterloo Toll-house** (SK 068357) 'T.G.' *Derby - Newcastle under Lyme*
A 'T.G.' marked on early OS maps is positioned in the junction of minor roads to Crakemarsh Hall and Spath, the site of this toll-house now a small roundabout.	Marked as a 'T.G.' on early OS maps a toll-house operated near Waterloo Farm, at the junction of Beamhurst Lane and the main road between Uttoxeter and Cheadle, present day A522.
It was probably the toll-gate cited in an Act of 1759 as being between the towns of Stramshall and Uttoxeter *'no closer than the Royal Oak'* and is not to be confused with the still surviving and elegant Crakemarsh Lodge further to the north.	It appears as 'Water Low' in the Census of 1861 and 10 years later was occupied by 63 year old widow and 'toll-gate keeper' Julia Cross, her daughter Mary Keen and a visitor recorded as William Ratcliff.

Hollington Toll-house, Checkley
SK 060388   'T.G.'
Cheadle - Rocester etc.

photo: tim jenkinson

This now rather heavily overbuilt toll -house still retains the name and stands in the village of Hollington near a small cross-roads, some three miles west of Rocester on the old road between there and Bearsbrook on the Stone to Uttoxeter turnpike (B 5027).

It is shown as a 'T.G.' on early 19th Century OS maps but the house retains few if any of its original features. There was probably a porch jutting into the road where the lower right window is now positioned. Built in c.1831 by the Cheadle Five Districts Trust it was occupied for a number of years by Stafford born Thomas Horobin who acted as the 'Gate Keeper' as well as being the local School Master.

Combridge Lane Toll-house
(SK 086388)   'T.G.'
Cheadle - Rocester etc.

A toll-gate is marked on early OS maps on what is now an unclassified road at the junction of Combridge Lane and Hollington Road approximately one mile west of Rocester.

Built on the Bearsbrook to Rocester turnpike by the Cheadle Five Districts Trust, 40 year old 'gate keeper' William Webster is at the house in 1861 with his wife Elizabeth and their five children. A nearby cast iron milepost at Woottons Farm, set up by the County Council after the turnpike era had ended, confirms the former importance of the road here.

Denstone Lane Toll-house, Alton
SK 083415   'T.G.'
Cheadle - Rocester etc.

photo: tim jenkinson

An Act of 1799 enabled the road from Cheadle through Alton to be turnpiked to its junction with the then Spath to Hanging Bridge road near Quixhill Bank in Denstone.

This rather plain brick built two storey toll-house, now 'Toll-gate Cottage', still stands in Denstone Lane at a rather isolated spot on the B3502 close to Micklin Farm near the village of Alton.

Currently unoccupied and somewhat dilapidated the house has a blocked doorway right at the road edge and two boarded windows, one each side. Built by the Cheadle Five Districts Turnpike Trust it was occupied in 1871 by 'Joiner's Labourer' George Leighton who may have doubled as the toll-collector. Its lack of listed status is a cause for concern given its current state of disrepair.

Counslow Toll-house, Cheadle
(SK 034427)   'T.G.'
Cheadle - Rocester etc.

Built about a mile and a half east of Cheadle town centre on the present day B5032, on what was part of the Cheadle to Quixhill Bank turnpike, a toll-house controlled minor roads crossing the major route at Counslow.

It appears in successive Census returns from 1871 as the 'Old Toll Bar' suggesting its abandonment by the Five Divisions Trust at that time.

Huntley Toll-house, Cheadle
SK 007411   'T.G.'
Sandon - Bullock Smithy etc.

photo: tim jenkinson

Built by the Cheadle Five Districts Turnpike Trust in c.1831 on a branch of the Sandon to Bullock Smithy Turnpike this impressive two storey toll-house stands about two miles from the town on the A522 towards Tean at the turn for Huntley.

Now grade II listed, it retains its angled frontage facing into the road, but has been considerably extended to the rear. Old photos show that the toll-house is actually brick built and at one time had a central chimney that has since been removed.

In 1861 the toll-collecting team of Sarah and Benjamin Kirkland were in residence with their four children.

Lower Tean Toll-house, Checkley
(SK 023383)   'T.G.'
Derby - Newcastle under Lyme

This toll-house was built in the parish of Checkley at Lower Tean under an Act of 1823 that accommodated three diversions to the main Newcastle to Derby turnpike.

It is shown as a 'T.G.' on early 19th Century OS maps and stood on what is now the A522 roughly midway between Uttoxeter and Cheadle.

Green Hill Toll-house, Cheadle
(SK 009438)   'T.G.'
Cheadle - Butterton Moor End

photo: staffordshire arts and muesum service

The first toll-house on the Cheadle to Butterton Moor End turnpike stood in the fork of two roads half a mile north of Cheadle. Here one road led north-west to Leek the other northwards down to Froghall Bridge at Green Hill. Rebuilt in 1836 at a cost of £67 (Sherlock 1976) by the Cheadle Five Districts Trust it appears from this old 1925 photograph to have actually been hexagonal in plan rather than the usual octagonal shape.

Marked as a 'T.G.' on old Ordnance Survey Maps, the toll-house was brick built with the porch edging into the road. It was recorded in 1871 as the 'Green Hill Toll-bar' and was occupied at that time by lone toll-collector Ann Berrisford. Nowadays a busy junction the house was probably demolished to improve visibility and access to the roads here.

Town End Toll-house, Cheadle
(SK 004432)   'T.G.'
Ashbourne - Leek etc.

Another of the Cheadle toll-houses once stood at the west end of the High Street, near its junction with present day Park Lane, an area known as Town End. It was built on part of the Blythe Marsh to Thorpe turnpike that dated from an Act of 1762 and was eventually consolidated with the Cheadle Five Districts Act of 1831.

Marked as a 'T.G.' on old OS maps, the toll-house was occupied in 1871 by 32 year old 'collector of tolls' Elizabeth James with her husband William and their six children.

Oakamoor Toll-house
(SK 054448)
Ashbourne - Leek etc.

photo: unknown

Another toll-house on the Blythe Marsh to Thorpe turnpike once stood adjacent to the Cricketer's Arms public house, just west of where two minor roads converge, in the village of Oakamoor. It was the first of several collecting points on the B5417 east of Cheadle heading towards Cotton and on into Derbyshire.

This old photograph taken during a parade through the village shows the toll-house to have been two storeys high with a gable end and doorway opening into the road. 32 year old 'gate keeper' Jessey Jackson and his 7 year old son Eli were living there in 1851. Although the pub still survives at the site there is no trace of the toll-house today.

Star Toll-house, Cotton
(SK 065456)
Ashbourne - Leek etc.

The next toll-gate on the B5417 was positioned in the village of Old Star, a mile north east of Oakamoor The name is attributable to the point where five roads converge and the toll-house most probably stood at that junction, near the present day Star Inn.

Built on the Blythe Marsh to Thorpe turnpike, it was occupied in 1871 by 59 year old 'Toll-gate tender' Mary Mellor and her 11 year old granddaughter Gertrude.

Three Lows Toll-house, Cotton
(SK 073467)
Ashbourne - Leek etc.

A toll-house once operated in the hamlet of Three Lows on the Blythe Marsh to Thorpe road dating from 1762. Built at or near the junction of the present day B5417 with an unclassified road that crosses towards Wootton, this toll-house has scant records, appearing only in the 1871 Census as the 'Old Toll-bar' at Three Lows with 52 year old 'Day Labourer' John Kidd in residence, and seemingly abandoned by then as a collecting point.

This photo dating from c.1960 shows the house to have been extended, possibly to form two dwellings with few features surviving from its turnpike days, so it is unclear as to why the house was later demolished.

Rue Hill Toll-house, Cauldon Lowe
(SK 084479)   'T.G.'
Ashbourne - Leek etc.

Appearing under the name of the 'Rock Toll-gate' in 1851 and 'Rue Hill Toll-bar' in 1871 this toll-house was in the hamlet of Cauldon Lowe close to the junction of the present day A52 with the B5417. It stood on the north side of the road besides a lane leading to Cauldon Grange and is referred to by Dodd and Dodd (1980) in *'Peakland Roads and Trackways'* implying that it has been demolished since then.

Built by the Blythe Marsh Turnpike Trust, the toll-house operated as one of the many on the road leading from the north Staffordshire town of Cheadle onto the moors and was occupied in 1871 by 'day labourer' John Clark and his family.

Stanton Dale Toll-house, Cotton
SK 109477
Ashbourne - Leek etc.

photo: tim jenkinson

Rebuilt in 1845 and bearing this date on a plaque high on the wall, the original Stanton Dale toll-house operated for the Blythe Marsh Turnpike Trust on the road via Cheadle to Thorpe in Derbyshire. It stood where its replacement now stands, at a junction where Dale Lane meets the present day A52.

Now with a blocked doorway and evidence of a porch at the roadside the 'new' two storey house went on to form part of the 'Cheadle Five Districts Trust' an amalgamation of local turnpikes on what was one of the least frequented and unprofitable routes in the county. Subsequently extended to the rear, the house appears simply as the 'Toll-gate' in the Census returns of 1871.

Calton Moor Toll-house
(SK 117488)   'T.G.'
Ashbourne - Leek etc.

Marked as a 'T.G.' on old OS maps of the area, this toll-house once stood in the hamlet of Calton Moor on the A52 Ashbourne to Leek road at its junction with what is now a minor road leading to Thorpe in Derbyshire.

Built by the Blythe Marsh Turnpike Trust in c.1762 the toll-house marshalled the route here along with the other gates at Stanton Dale, Blore crossroads and in Spend (Spen) Lane in Thorpe itself.

Wootton Toll-house, Ellastone
SK 105451   'T.G.'
Darley Moor - Ellastone etc.

photo: tim jenkinson

Some 12 miles from Leek, a toll-house was built in the village of Wootton on the unclassified road between Ellastone and Three Lows, originally part of the Darley Moor to Winkhill Bank turnpike. Close to the Derbyshire border and recorded as within that county in the Census of 1851, it was then occupied by 'Toll Gate Collector' William Salt, his wife Anne and their three young children all aged under five years.

The house is marked as a 'T.G.' on early OS maps at a position where a large two storey house 'Tollgate Cottage' now stands opposite Tollgate House, at the junction with Hall Lane. Whilst the frontage does edge onto the road, there are no other discernible features remaining from its toll-collecting days.

Waterhouses Toll-house, Calton
(SK 094500)   'T.G.'
Ashbourne - Leek etc.

An Act of 1762 permitted a turnpike from Ashbourne in Derbyshire over the Staffordshire border at Hanging Bridge and onwards through Mayfield and Waterhouses to the town of Leek. Abandoned by the Trust in 1881, the toll-house at Waterhouses appears as the 'Old toll-gate' in the Census of that year, occupied by 23 year old 'washer woman' Emma Robinson and her 3 year old daughter Sarah.

Marked as a 'T.G.' on early 19th Century OS maps the toll-house was about half a mile east of the village, just west of where a minor road from Calton joins the present day A523.

Ellastone Road Toll-house, Upper Cotton
SK 061488   'T.G.'
Darley Moor - Ellastone etc.

photo: tim jenkinson

Set on part of the Darley Moor to Winkhill Bank turnpike, this two storey toll-house stands on Ellastone Road in Upper Cotton at a rather remote spot to the north-west of Windy Harbour. It was built at a junction where an old road leads north-west to the old toll-gate at Ipstones Edge on the Cheadle to Butterton Moor End road.

A porch and doorway and latterly a window have been removed from the wall at the roadside where a toll-board would probably have been affixed. Extended to the rear since the 1950's the house once operated for the Darley Moor and Ellastone Turnpike Trust and appears as the 'Cotton Toll-Gate' in the Census of 1861 with 'Labourer' Samuel Wakefield and his family in residence.

Kingsley Holt Toll-house
(SK 019461)
Cheadle - Butterton Moor End

This toll-house was built on the Cheadle to Butterton Moor End turnpike in the village of Kingsley Holt two miles north of Cheadle where present day Shawe Park Road becomes Churnet Valley Road.

In 1871 the lone occupant of the house was 62 year old 'Gate tender' Fanny Pratt. A nearby cast iron milepost recording distances to several destinations confirms the importance of the route here.

High Street Toll-house, Ipstones
SK 023502   'T.G.'
Cheadle - Butterton Moor End

photo: tim jenkinson

An Act of 1769 sanctioned a turnpike from Green Hill in Cheadle north through Kingsley Holt and Ipstones to Bottom House, on the Ashbourne to Leek road, and then on through the village of Onecote as far as Butterton Moor End.

A typically angle fronted two storey toll-house was built at the top of High Street in Ipstones, at its junction with Park Lane.   Now rendered and extended to the side, old photos show that it was originally brick built with a porch edging to the roadside.   Still known as 'The Old Toll-house', successive Census returns show it simply as the 'Toll-gate' occupied in 1851 by 'Barr Keeper' Mary Cope and her 18 year old 'dress maker' daughter Jane.   The three bedroom property was recently on the market in 2010 for £275,000.

Froghall Bridge Toll-house
(SK 025471)   'T.G.'
Cheadle - Butterton Moor End

A new bridge at Froghall was built in accordance with the 1769 Act to facilitate passage over the River Churnet on the road from Cheadle to Butterton Moor End.   A toll-gate is marked at or near the bridge on early 19th Century OS maps.

The Census returns of 1861 record the Minshall family as living there with 46 year old Catherine, wife of Railway labourer William, identified as the 'Toll-gate Keeper'.   By 1881 John Lane a 'labourer in the Limestone Works' is at 'Froghall Toll Gate House' with his wife Emma, but by then the house was probably no longer being used by the Cheadle Five Districts Turnpike Trust.

Windy Harbour Toll-house, Ipstones Edge
SK 028512
Cheadle - Butterton Moor End

Surprisingly this small two storey square stone built toll-house still stands on the west side of the crossroads at Ipstones Edge, but now considerably altered it adjoins a much larger building to the north. By the time of this 1926 photograph it had fallen into disrepair, but can be seen to have once had a doorway and small porch projecting to the road edge.

Operating on what was then the Cheadle to Butterton Moor Turnpike at the junction with a road south east to Windy Harbour, it was probably built c.1831 by the Cheadle Five Districts Trust. Little more than a mile from the High Street toll-gate in the village, the house was occupied in 1871 by 'Toll-gate tender' Ann Thompson and her family.

Moor End Toll-house, Butterton
(SK 059563)
Cheadle - Butterton Moor End

The location of this now demolished toll-house is unclear, but turnpike records show that a gate once operated at 'Moor End', a name given to a hamlet about a mile north of the village of Onecote. The Cheadle to Butterton Moor End turnpike was set up in 1769 and the house was probably positioned on what is now the present day B5053, at the junction where a minor road leads south-east to Grindon.

The toll-house is recorded in the Census returns of 1871 with 'collector at the gate' identified as a Mrs Grundy living there with her husband Thomas and their two children. Records of toll collections at Moor End from 1817-1824 are still held at Stafford Record Office.

Onecote Toll-house
SK 049551
Cheadle - Butterton Moor End

photo: tim jenkinson

It is possible that this small stone built house on the current B5053, 6 miles from Leek and 4 from Ipstones, was once used to collect tolls in the village of Onecote, on the former Cheadle to Butterton Moor End road, turnpiked in 1769. It stands beside the 'Old Post Office', opposite Douse Lane that leads to Bradnop, and seems nowadays to be used as a store.

It retains a chimney and has blocked windows and a modified doorway on the roadside, all suggestive of its former role. Recorded as the 'Toll-gate house' in the village in 1861 with 'Carpenter Master' George Gibson and his family in residence it was probably his wife Martha who was acting as the 'toll-keeper' at that time. Ten years later, the 'Toll-gate' is occupied by 42 year old 'agricultural labourer' John Higton and family.

Brownlow Toll-house, Warslow
(SK 074577)   'T.G.'
Butterton Moor End - Buxton etc.

A toll-house was built a mile south-west of Warslow on what is now the B5053 Cheadle to Buxton road, to the south of a minor road leading to Lower and Upper Elkstone.

Operating on part of what was then the Butterton Moor End to Buxton turnpike, it was recorded as the 'Brownlow Gate' in the 1871 Census. Along with the nearby Dale Gate, Brownlow was one of the toll-houses included in a 'season ticket' issued from 1817 that would clear all gates on this road leading from Butterton Moor to Hartington Mill Lane in Derbyshire.

Hulme End Toll-house, Sheen
SK 106593   'T.G.'
Butterton Moor End - Buxton etc.

photo: tim jenkinson

This small single storey square stone built toll-house still stands on the present day B5054, near the border with Derbyshire. It is in the hamlet of Hulme End, on the east side of the bridge over the River Manifold and opposite the public house of the same name.

Built in c.1791 by the Butterton, Warslow, Hartington and Longnor Turnpike Trust the house worked the turnpike and river ford simultaneously on the Oils Heath to Newhaven route.

Appearing in the Parish of Sheen in the Census returns of 1871 as the 'Hulme End Toll-gate' it was occupied at that time by 'toll-collector' Margaret Ward and her 11 year old son William.

Dale Toll-house, Warslow
(SK 092587)
Butterton Moor End - Buxton etc.

The Butterton Moor End to Buxton road was turnpiked in 1770 and passed through the village of Warslow heading north towards Longnor. A second toll-house known as 'Dale' operated just east of the village on a branch road that led to Hulme End and then the Derbyshire border. This toll-house along with the nearby Brownlow Gate is recorded as undergoing repairs in turnpike records from 1827-31.

63 year old 'Toll-gate keeper' and widow Mary Bradley lived at the house in 1851 with her two sons Joseph and Thomas. By 1861, 76 year old Matthew Birch with his wife and family had taken on the toll-collecting role.

Crowdecote Toll-house (Derbys)
SK 101651
Newcastle under Lyme - Hassop etc.

photo: tim jenkinson

Built about a mile to the east of Longnor on a branch of the Newcastle to Hassop turnpike at the county border this picturesque toll-house stands in the village of Crowdecote in Derbyshire.

Now 'Tollbar Cottage' the toll-house adjoins a larger house and retains its windows and doorway facing towards the stone bridge over the River Dove that dates from 1709 and was built to replace what was then a wooden footbridge at 'Crowdy Coat'.

Tolls ceased to be collected from this point on November 1st 1873.

> **Titterton Toll-house, Sheen**
> (SK 111595)
> *Butterton Moor End - Buxton etc.*
>
> The Warslow to Hartington road was turnpiked in 1770 as part of the Butterton Moor End to Buxton turnpike and was later realigned to cross the River Manifold at Hulme End, where a toll-house operated from c.1791. That building still survives and a second toll-house was built c.1840 just half a mile towards Hartington at the junction of a minor road leading south to Alstonefield on what is now the B5054.
>
> In 1851 the second house, known as the 'Titterton Gate', was occupied by 50 year old 'Toll-collector and school mistress' Jane Mellor, her son and nephew. Ten years later the role had been taken over by 40 year old Margaret Ward living there with her four children. The road through Hulme End was disturnpiked in 1878.

Bridge Toll-house, Quarnford
SK 004664
Newcastle under Lyme - Hassop etc.

photo: tim jenkinson

This two storey toll-house was built on a branch of the Newcastle to Hassop turnpike as late as 1842 on the north side of a T junction in the Parish of Quarnford at 'Greens' in part of the North Staffordshire Peak District. It replaced the nearby Goldsitch Moss toll-gate and probably once had a porch and doorway on the wall facing into the road with space above for a toll-board, both of which have since been replaced by windows.

The house which was considerably extended to the sides in 1990 is often enveloped in creeper during the summer months. It had a relatively short life collecting tolls being abandoned by the Trust after just ten years in 1852 (British History Online) but it still retains the name of 'Toll-bridge Cottage'.

Bridge Toll-house, Longnor
(SK 088643)   'T.G.'
Butterton Moor End - Buxton etc.

Another toll-house was erected to the north of 'Windy Harbor Cottage' (now The Cottage) in the fork of two roads on part of the main Cheadle to Buxton road, the present day B5053.

This road was first constructed via Longnor in 1770 and the toll-gate probably dated from that time.

28 year old 'toll-collector' Jane Naden, her husband and three young children are living at the house in 1871. The Trust disbanded in around 1878 freeing this road of tolls.

Goldsitch Moss Toll-house, Quarnford
SK 006659   'T.G.'
Newcastle under Lyme - Hassop etc.

photo: tim jenkinson

An Act of 1773 covered a branch of the Leek to Longnor road along what was then the Newcastle to Hassop turnpike passing through Goldsitch Moss and Quarnford. This small and rather indistinct single storey oblong stone built toll-house stands on a minor road opposite the house known as 'Bradley Howel'.

Built in 1825 to replace the nearby Gib Torr toll-gate, the house appears in the 1851 Census as the 'Goldsitch Moss Toll-Bar' with 61 year old 'Retired Coal Miner' Abel Goodwin, his wife Sarah their daughter and grandson in residence. By then, although still retaining the name, it had been replaced by the building of a new toll-house to the north at 'Greens' in Quarnock and was no longer being used by the Trust.

Town End Toll-house, Longnor
(SK 087647)   'T.G.'
Newcastle under Lyme - Hassop

The Newcastle to Hassop turnpike via the village of Longnor was built in around 1765 and a gate and toll-house stood just to the north of Longnor Bridge over the River Manifold from 1775.

Appearing as the 'Town End Toll-Bar' in the Census returns of 1871 with 'Toll-bar keeper' Hannah Berresford and her family at the house, the road was eventually disturnpiked in 1875 and the house was probably demolished not long thereafter.

Nabs Chain Toll-house, Heathylee
SK 019619
Newcastle under Lyme - Hassop etc.

photo: tim jenkinson

Built in around 1842 to replace an earlier toll-gate at the site on what is now the A53 Leek to Buxton road on Leek Moor, Naychurch this rectangular toll-house stills stands below the impressive Ramshaw Rocks at the junction of a minor road leading up to Goldsitch Moss.

The toll-house with a low window facing into the road appears under the name of the 'Nabs Chain Toll-gate, Heathylee' in the Census returns of 1871 with 66 year old 'Toll -collector and Button Maker' Sarah Goodwin living there with her 10 year old granddaughter Mary Jane Bickford. This may be the point that is also referred to as 'Mile Tree' in various turnpike and historical records.

Flash Bar Toll-house, Quarnford
(SK 032678)   'T.G.'
Newcastle under Lyme - Hassop etc.

This toll-house dated from c.1771 and was built at the junction of a road going south east to Longnor on what is the present day A53 to the north east of Flash.

Marked as 'T.G.' on early 19th Century OS maps, the toll-house is known to have also had a side bar into an adjoining road. Still in evidence in 1841 it appeared under the name of 'Flash Gate', when it was being used to collect tolls on part of the Newcastle to Hassop Turnpike on the road between Leek and Buxton in Derbyshire.

Leek Edge Toll-house, Leek
SJ 998573   'T.G.'
Newcastle under Lyme - Hassop etc.

photo: tim jenkinson

Now rather heavily extended and overbuilt, this nonetheless attractive two storey house once served as a toll-gate operating for the Leek and Hassop, Middlehills and Buxton Turnpike Trust.

It stands at Leek Edge, about half a mile from the town on the road towards Derbyshire, the present day A53, at its junction with Thorncliff Road.

The toll-house, now 'Waste Cottage', has been extended to the side and rear and possesses a bay window facing the road as well as blocked doorway. It was occupied in 1871 by 55 year old 'stone mason' Samuel Billing his daughter and wife Elizabeth who was acting in the capacity of the 'Toll-gate keeper'.

Gib Torr Toll-house, Quarnford
(SK 012650)
Newcastle under Lyme - Hassop

This toll-house was constructed in c.1775 at the time of a new turnpike running along a side road leading from Royal Cottage via Gib Torr to the Manor Farm in Quarnford.

At this site for some 50 years, the toll-house and its gate were eventually replaced by the Goldsitch Moss toll-gate that was built beside the house of John Bradley, known as 'Bradley Howel'.

Lowe Hill Toll-house, Leek
SJ 994561
Ashbourne - Leek etc.

photo: tim jenkinson

The Leek to Ashbourne Turnpike was completed in 1762 and a toll-house was built at Lowe Hill c.1765, less than a mile from the town. It was used for the collection of tolls for over 60 years, before being sold and replaced by another toll-gate near Bradnop, following an improvement to the line of the road.

Described as late as 1960 as surviving as part of a house, it is possible that this is the building in question, an extended two storey brick built cottage in Ashbourne Road opposite Moorland Road. It retains a low window facing into the highway, that may have been a former doorway. In the 1871 Census it actually appears as the 'Lowe Hill Old Gate House'.

Middle Hills Toll-house, Heathylee
(SK 027639)
Newcastle under Lyme - Hassop etc.

The main road between Leek and Buxton was laid out in the late 1760s as part of the Newcastle to Hassop turnpike. A 'Middle Hills Toll-Gate' was first set up in 1773 and is recorded in the Census returns of 1871 for Heathylee.
This may be the toll-house that is known to have operated to the south of Royal Cottage just off the main Leek to Buxton road, controlling what is a side road leading eastward into the village of Longnor. At the time of the Census 48 year old 'toll-collector' Mary Downes is living at the house with her 'shoemaker' husband Abraham.

Four Lost Leek Toll-houses

Sandon - Bullock Smithy etc.

Pool End Toll-house, Leek
(SJ 967581)
Sandon - Bullock Smithy etc.

The toll-house at Pool End was built in 1824 to replace an older house at Packsaddle near Rudyard Manor, that had stood on the Sandon to Bullock Smithy turnpike between Leek and Macclesfield in Cheshire since 1762. The new toll-house was positioned about two miles north-west of Leek, where the B5331 joins the A523, and was occupied in 1871 by 48 year old 'Toll-gate keeper' Samuel Birch, his wife Mary and their two children James and Mary.

Sheephouse Toll-gate, Leek
(SJ 986540)   'T.G.'
Sandon - Bullock Smithy etc.

Originally built in 1762 on the road to Cheddleton (A520) near to Sheephouse Farm, this toll-house is shown as a 'T.G.' on early OS maps at the junction of a minor road leading south to Leekbrook. Initially it seems that this was an unpopular site as in 1763 Toll-keeper John Sutton was assaulted and the Trust gave him £1 compensation and £3 for repair of the windows (Longton Thomas, 1934).
The 1861 Census records 45 year old widow and 'Toll-collector' Margaret Gillman at the house with her eight children. The road was disturnpiked in 1878 and the house was subsequently put up for sale by the outgoing Trust.

Pool Hall Toll-house, Bradnop
(SK 004555)   'T.G.'
Ashbourne - Leek etc.

Built c.1828 to replace the Lowe Hill toll-gate and demolished as late as the 1970's this toll-house stood on the east side of the present day A523 about two miles south-east of Leek at a turn to Wild Goose Farm.
It was occupied in 1861 by 56 year old 'Toll-gates keeper' Jane Birch and two boarders, John and Christina Hages. By 1871 'Shoemaker and toll-collector' John Stevenson is recorded at the house with his 12 year old daughter Elizabeth. The road was disturnpiked in 1876.

Wall Bridge Toll-house,
(SJ 974552)   'T.P.'   **Ladderedge**
Newcastle under Lyme - Hassop

This toll-house was just south of Wall Bridge over the River Churnet at Ladderedge, and replaced an earlier tollgate 'T.G.' that was positioned c.1765 near the canal wharf on the Newcastle Road out of Leek (SJ 980560).
At a more accessible point on this important road, the toll-house at Wall Bridge was built around 1855 and is recorded in the Census returns of 1871 with 63 year old 'Tailor and toll-collector' John Naylor in residence with his wife Ellen and their teenage son John, a mere eight years before the Trust was disbanded.

Blakeley Lane Toll-house, Dilhorne
(SJ 976470)
Shelton - Cauldon etc.

Operating in the hamlet of Blakeley Lane on a section of the present day A52, this two storey building was shown as one of the county's surviving toll-houses by Robert Sherlock in 1976. An Act of 1771 turnpiked the route from Shelton via Bucknall and Cellarhead, to Blakeley Lane End, to join the Cheadle to Leek route.

Rather plain and white washed, 'Tollgate Cottage' was demolished as recently as 2009 to make way for a new house and driveway at the site. This photo taken shortly before its demise shows its position close to the highway edge, with two low windows facing into the road and a side door which may have once have had a porch in the gable end. The continuing threat to Staffordshire's road heritage is self evident from this toll-house's disappearance.

Heath House Toll-gate,
(SJ 967506)   'T.G.   **Cheddleton**
Sandon - Bullock Smithy etc.

Marked as a 'T.G.' on early 19th Century OS maps, this toll-house was positioned near the junction of Felthouse Lane with the present day A520, about a mile north of Wetley Rocks on the approach towards Cheddleton. The road here was turnpiked in 1762.

In 1861 the toll-house appears under the name of 'Heath House' and was occupied by 60 year old widow and 'Turnpike Toll Collector' Elizabeth Wellon, her son and daughter. Ten years later 'Agricultural labourer' David Blakeman is at the house with his 26 year old wife and 'toll-gate keeper' Ann.

Four More Lost Toll-houses

Newcastle - Hassop etc.

Endon Toll-house
(SJ 925533)   'T.G.'
Newcastle under Lyme - Hassop

A toll-house operated on what is now the A53 in Endon, on the Newcastle to Hassop turnpike, at a place known as the 'Fountain' at the junction with a side road from Stanley (Keele University 1974). A 'T.G.' is shown on old OS maps just south-west of the main part of Endon village.

Built in 1767, two years after the road was first turnpiked, the toll-house stood on the opposite corner to the present day Methodist Chapel and was still being used for collecting tolls in 1871 when 56 year old 'toll-collector' Catherine Marshall and her 17 year old daughter and 'assistant' Elizabeth were living there. Tolls ceased to be collected on November 1st 1873.

Stockton Brook Toll-house,
(SJ 917521)   **Bagnall**
Newcastle under Lyme - Hassop

Another toll-house was built near enough in the centre of the village of Stockton Brook on the New Leek Road (A53), the turnpike between Newcastle under Lyme and Hassop in Derbyshire.

It dated from around 1828 when this part of the road was completed between Stoke and Leek, but the date of its demolition is unknown.

Sandon - Bullock Smithy

Hugbridge Toll-house, Rushton
(SJ 932631)   'T.G.'   **Spencer**
Sandon - Bullock Smithy etc.

A 'T.G.' is marked on early 19th Century OS maps about half a mile south of the county border at Hugbridge over the River Dane. Built in 1826 on the Sandon to Bullock Smithy turnpike, it replaced an earlier gate that had stood at the bridge.
The toll-house was occupied in 1871 by 36 year old 'labourer at the chemical works' William Cook and his family. This road across the county border was disturnpiked in 1878 and the house was probably demolished not long thereafter, along with another a mile closer to Macclesfield at the junction with Tunstall Road, just south of the Cheshire village of Bosley.

Ryecroft Gate Toll-house,
(SJ 939616)   **Rushton Spencer**
Sandon - Bullock Smithy etc.

This toll-house probably stood at the crossroads in the hamlet of Ryecroft Gate about half a mile south of Rushton Spencer on the Sandon to Bullock Smithy turnpike between Leek and Macclesfield, the present day A523.
It appears as the 'Rushton Spencer Toll-gate' in the Census returns of 1871 with 63 year old Cheshire born 'toll-gate keeper' James Moss his two adult daughters and three grand children in residence.

Withystakes Toll-house, Werrington
SJ 948477   'T.G.'
Shelton - Cauldon etc.

photo: tim jenkinson

Built on the corner of present day Rownall Road and Armshead Road in the village of Werrington, this toll-house is still known to this day as 'Tollbar Cottage' and underwent considerable renovation in 2011. It once collected tolls on what was part of the Shelton to Blakeley Lane End turnpike that further east joined the road between Cheadle and Leek.

Built by the Cheadle Turnpike Trust in the early 19th Century and marked as 'T.G.' on early OS maps, it is fairly typical of two storey foursquare toll-houses, retaining a characteristic porch projecting to the road edge, with a small window in the side wall facing the junction, all indicative of its former role.

Stone Walls Toll-house, Dilhorne
(SJ 971456)   'T.G.'
Forsbrook - Cheddleton

Another toll-house was positioned about a mile and a half north of Dilhorne in the hamlet of Stone Walls on the road between Forsbrook and Cheddleton.

Like the Sarver Lane toll-house in Dilhorne village, this was similarly abandoned at the time of the new toll-house build in Forsbrook in 1838. It was nonetheless marked as a 'T.G.' on OS maps of the early 19th Century, but nothing remains at the site today to suggest there was ever a building there.

Four Lost Toll-houses East of Newcastle

Derby - Newcastle under Lyme

The Foley Toll-house, Fenton
(approx SJ 907438)   **Culvert**
Derby - Newcastle under Lyme

Still extant in 1960 at The Foley on the Longton Boundary, this toll-house was described as 'a small gabled cottage on the south side of the road' (British History Online) and effectively sealed off the approach to Longton from the west.

The area of The Foley is described as being 'wholly in Fenton Culvert' by John Ward in 1843 and the toll-house seems to have built somewhere in the Longton end of King Street. Extensive demolition of old buildings took place here in 1983 and that may be when the toll-house was lost.

Meir Toll-house
(SJ 931422)   'T.G.'
Derby - Newcastle under Lyme

Appearing as 'T.G.' on early 19th Century OS maps, the original toll-gate at Mear (Meir) was set up around the time of the Derby to Newcastle road being turnpiked there in 1759.

Still operational in 1871 with 56 year old 'Toll-gate keeper' Thomas Poole at the toll-house with his wife Elizabeth and their five children, the area has been greatly developed in recent times and a large roundabout now dominates this junction where the A520 crosses the A50 between Stoke upon Trent and Uttoxeter.

Draycott in the Moors Toll-house
(SJ 985400)
Derby - Newcastle under Lyme

A toll-house is recorded in successive mid 19th Century Census returns located in Draycott in the Moors, probably just to the south of the village on the old Roman Road that once formed part of the main Newcastle to Derby turnpike via Blythe Marsh and Uttoxeter.
Occupied in both 1861 and 1871 by 'labourer on the turnpike' Joseph Keene and his wife Jane it had previously been inhabited in 1851 by 36 year old 'labourer on roads and toll-gate collector' Jesse Rowley, his wife Mary and their four children.

Totmonslow Toll-house, Draycott
(SJ 988398)   'T.G.'
Derby - Newcastle under Lyme

Census returns of 1861 also indicate a second toll-gate in the village of Draycott in the Moors, the two in close proximity, operating on the stretch of turnpike road between Blythe Marsh and Uttoxeter.

The toll-house at Totmonslow is marked as a 'T.G.' on early 19th Century OS maps and stood just outside the village at the junction of a minor road leading to Cresswell. It was occupied in 1861 by 'agricultural labourer' John Watson, his wife Elizabeth and their three children.

Forsbrook Toll-house, Dilhorne
(SJ 966416)
Ashbourne - Leek etc.

photo: staffordshire record office

Built in 1838 at a cost of £18 10 shillings by the Cheadle Turnpike Trust this toll-house stood at the corner of Dilhorne and Cheadle Roads in Forsbrook until its unfortunate demolition in 1959 for road widening.

This old photograph from around that time shows that the two storey brick built toll-house had a projecting front and blocked window above the doorway where a toll-board was probably once fixed.

Recorded in 1861 as 'Toll-gate house Cheadle Lane', with 31 year old 'Potter and hardware presser' Thomas Adams at the house, it is probably his wife Ann who was acting as the toll-collector at that time. The Trust disbanded in 1878 and the house was then sold into private ownership.

Sarver Lane Toll-house,
(SJ 974436) 'T.G.' **Dilhorne**
Forsbrook - Cheddleton

An Act of 1790 turnpiked the road from Forsbrook northwards through Dilhorne to join the Cheadle to Leek turnpike near Blakeley Lane End.

A toll-house was first built in Dilhorne at the junction of Sarver Lane with present day High Street, but the coming of the new Forsbrook toll-house in 1838 saw the demise of this collection point. To this day there is a brick built two storey house with small lean to porch standing in the fork of the two roads, but its role in the turnpike era cannot be confirmed.

Four Lost Caverswall and Normacot Toll-houses

Sandon - Bullock Smithy etc.

Adderley Green Toll-house,
(SJ 921449)   'T.G.'   **Caverswall**
Shelton - Cauldon etc.

A branch of the Shelton to Cauldon turnpike running from Bucknall to Weston Coyney passed through Adderley Green from 1813. Marked as a 'T.G'. on early 19th Century OS maps, a toll-house was built about a mile to the west of the Weston Coyney Gate on the south side of the road, the present day A5272.

It appeared as 'Mossfields Toll-gate house' in 1851 with Abbots Bromley born 'toll-collector' Elizabeth Gee and her 'Turnpike Road Labourer' husband William, their daughter and niece at the house. By 1871 it is recorded as 'Adderley Green Toll-house' with 58 year old 'toll-collector' Frances Brough living there with her husband William and their two teenage children.

Lightwood Toll-house,
(SJ 925414)   'T.G.'   **Normacot**
Stone - Longton etc.

Appearing under the name of 'Gravelly Bank' in 1841, this toll-house was built just north of the junction of Lightwood Road with the present day A5005. It was occupied in 1871 by 'carpenter and toll-collector' James Marsh living there with his wife Mary Ann their two young sons and his sister -in-law, Hannah Hand.

Weston Coyney Toll-house,
(SJ 934439)   'T.G.'   **Caverswall**
Sandon - Bullock Smithy etc.

This toll-house was positioned about a mile west of the village of Caverswall, where the road from Bucknall joined the Sandon to Leek road.

It was occupied in 1861 by 26 year old 'Toll-collector' Sarah Ann Bloore and her labourer husband Samuel. In 1871 it was recorded as the 'Weston Road Toll-gate House'. Much extended and altered after the turnpike era, it later became known as the 'Cross Roads House', but was demolished in the 1950's for road widening at the junction.

Meir Heath Toll-house, Normacot
(SJ 929401)   'T.G.'
Sandon - Bullock Smithy etc.

The Meir Heath toll-house controlled the junction where the Stone to Blythe Bridge road crossed the Sandon to Leek road, about two miles south of Meir village, a junction now comprising two mini-roundabouts.

Shown as 'T.G.' on early OS maps and 'Normacot T.P.' on the 1:2500 OS map of c.1880, it was occupied in 1871 by the toll-collecting team of William and Emma Gilbert and their four year old daughter Mary Ann. Another 'T.G.' is shown to the south of here on early 19th Century maps positioned on what is now the B5066 to Sandon at SJ 930399.

Barlaston Road Toll-house, Blurton
(SJ 899415)   'T.G.'
Stone - Longton etc.

photo: warrillow collection, keele university library

The 1771 Act of Parliament for the Stone to Longton turnpike also included a road running west from Meir, now the A5035, through Trentham to Stableford Bridge on the Stone to Woore road. Early 19th Century OS maps show a 'T.G.' set on the corner of Barlaston Road, about half a mile south of Blurton. This old photograph from c.1900 seems to show the toll-house as a tall two storey building with a gabled front and signs that it once had a porch facing into the road.

Coming from Longton, it would have controlled the route into both Trentham and Barlaston to the south. Appearing simply as the 'toll-gate' in the Census of 1861 it was occupied at that time by 'toll-collector' Ann Addison, her 'agricultural labourer' husband Samuel and her unmarried 'dressmaker' sister Martha Chatterley. The house was known locally as the 'Gingerbread' Toll-gate.

Hem Heath Toll-house,
(SJ 879410)   'T.G.'   **Trentham**
Stone - Longton etc.

Further along the road to the west of the Blurton Toll-gate another toll-house operated at Hem Heath, less than a mile from Trentham at or near the bridge over the present day Trent and Mersey Canal.

It appears in the Census of 1861 as '53, Hem Heath' with Samuel and Anne Halmarack recorded as the 'tollgate keepers'. The waterway at this time was known as the 'Grand Trunk Canal'.

Five Lost Fenton and Bucknall Toll-houses

Shelton - Cauldon etc. Derby - Newcastle under Lyme

Bucknall New Road Toll-house
(SJ 893476)   'T.G.'
Shelton - Cauldon etc.

Built c.1831 at the junction of the Old and New Bucknall Road in Hanley, this toll-house was known locally as the 'Ivy House Gate'. Still standing in 1871, the Census records 'toll-collector' Joseph Ramsden and his wife Ann there. Today the site is marked by a granite drinking trough.

The Act of 1771 also included a branch from Bucknall to Weston Coyney on the Sandon to Leek road. Old OS maps show a 'T.G.' just south of Townsend in Bucknall (SJ 905472), which along with another toll-gate in the village of Abbey Hulton (SJ 905487) would have controlled the north-south route through Bucknall, the latter set on part of the 1840 route from Hanley to the Endon toll-gate on the Newcastle to Leek turnpike road (present day A53).

Bridge Toll-house
(SJ 894473)
Bridge Trust

A gate operated on Ivy House Road a short distance south of the Bucknall New Road toll-house. 44 year old 'toll-collector' Henry Sims is recorded there in the 1871 Census, with his wife Mary and their five children.
It is not clear whether Henry was working for the turnpike or the canal authorities, but today the site has just a draw-bridge over the canal, the house and gates long since removed.

High Street Toll-house, Fenton
(SJ 886448)   'T.G.'
Derby - Newcastle under Lyme

Built in c.1832 near where present day Napier Street joins City Road just west of Fenton, this toll-house appears in the Census returns of 1851 in the ecclesiastical district of Christ Church, with 24 year old 'toll-gate keeper' Henry Sims with his wife, young daughter and mother living there.
The road here was disturnpiked in 1875 and later declared a highway with County Council responsibility under the Highways and Locomotives Act of 1878 (British History Online).

Heron Cross Toll-house,
(SJ 894438)   **Great Fenton**
Derby - Newcastle under Lyme

Under the Derby to Newcastle Turnpike Act of 1759, a toll-gate was erected at Heron Cross in Great Fenton at the junction of Heron Street with Duke Street, a little to the south of the present day A50.
Subsequently a toll-house was built at the site and is recorded as such in the Census returns of 1861 with 61 year old 'toll-gate keeper' and widow Elizabeth Alcock in residence with her 14 year old 'potter painter' granddaughter Elizabeth Appleton. The 1:2500 OS map of 1878 shows it as 'Longton Lane T.P.' with a bar controlling the road to the west.

Cauldon Place Toll-house, Stoke on Trent
SJ 878462   'T.G.'
Newcastle under Lyme - Hassop etc.

photo: tim jenkinson

Appearing as a 'T.G.' on early OS maps and now used as a newsagent's shop that retains the name 'Tollgate', this two storey toll-house stands on the Stoke Road, near to Shelton opposite Cauldon Road. It was built in about 1806 about a quarter of a mile north of Shelton Wharf on what is the present day A5006.

The toll-house clearly stands forward into the road, unlike the terraces either side that were built much later and it may have once had a porch where the doorway now is. It rather misleadingly appears as the 'Leek New Road toll-house' in the Census of 1871 with 48 year old 'Tailor and toll-collector' John Tunnicliffe in residence along with his wife Mary and their seven children.

Etruria Vale Road Toll-house
(SJ 874469)   'T.G.'
Newcastle under Lyme - Hassop

By 1832 another toll-gate had been set up at the southern end of Etruria Vale Road on the slope between Sun Street and Rectory Road.

It is shown as a 'T.G.' on early OS maps of the area and along with the houses at Cobridge, Cauldon Place and Etruria village would have effectively sealed off all of the western approaches leading into Hanley.

Four Lost Hanley Toll-houses

Newcastle under Lyme - Hassop etc.

Etruria Toll-house, Stoke Upon Trent
(SJ 872475)   'T.G.'
Newcastle under Lyme - Hassop etc.

There was a toll-house on the Newcastle to Hassop turnpike near the junction of Etruria Vale Road with the present day A53, Cobridge Road. Forming the northern boundary of the township of Penkhull this stretch of road was regularly in such a poor state of repair that in 1780 it was reported that despite considerable expenditure 'post chaises from Newcastle Under Lyme to Leek go by another road, two miles longer' (British History Online).
Built around 1832 the toll-house was occupied in 1851 by 52 year old 'Agent to Toll-contractor' and widower William Hilton, his five children and grandson whilst three doors away is John Blood the 'Toll-gate keeper' living with his housekeeper Mary Wilcox and her three children.   By 1871 the house had become known as the 'Lord Street Toll-gate', and in 1904 it was taken down upon the laying out of Etruria Park.

Brook Street Toll-house
(SJ 874481)
Newcastle under Lyme - Hassop etc.

This toll-house stood about half a mile north of the Etruria toll-gate at the junction of what was then Boothen Lane (now Century Street) with part of the main Newcastle to Leek route on the Cobridge Road, the present day A53.
Built around 1799 the toll-house was occupied in 1871 by lone 'toll-collector' 65 year old Hannah Astbury.

Keelings Lane Toll-house,
(SJ 887484)   **Upper Green**
Tunstall - Bosley etc.

Extensive building took place in the Keelings Lane area of Hanley in 1775 and later a toll-house stood near the point where it meets Town Road in an old part of the town known as Upper Green.
Along with another gate in nearby Hulton Street the house managed the route south and west into Northwood and was recorded in 1861 simply as the 'turnpike, Keelings Lane' with 'potter' James Nixon and his wife Eliza in residence.

Hope Street Toll-house
(SJ 880482)
Newcastle under Lyme - Hassop

Recorded under this name in the 1871 Census with 40 year old 'toll-gate keeper' William Jackson, his wife May and their seven sons living there, this toll-house, probably dating from around 1832, stood at the Vale Place end of Waterloo Road at or near the junction of York and Hope Street on what is the present day A50.
It is likely that this was one of the newer toll-gates on seven turnpikes that were sanctioned by a turnpike Act of 1828 in the Cobridge, Etruria and Shelton district.

Cobridge Toll-house, Burslem
(SJ 875487)   'T.G.'
Newcastle under Lyme - Hassop etc.

photo: warrillow collection, keele university library

This old photograph from the Warrillow collection, held at Keele University Library, dates from c.1880 and shows on the right hand side the distinctive toll-house that once stood at the junction of Waterloo Road and Grange Street in Burslem. The seemingly diminutive two storey building was built c.1832 and marshalled the western end of the road to Sneyd Green Colliery along Sneyd Street, where another gate was positioned.

It appeared in the 1861 Census returns under the name of 'Waterloo Toll-Gate' with 59 year old 'Toll-gate keeper' John Lovatt, his wife Martha and their 'tailor' son William at the address.

Hot Lane Toll-house, Burslem
(SJ 875494)
Newcastle under Lyme - Hassop etc.

A toll-house was positioned at the junction of Nile Street and Hot Lane in Burslem from 1832 to cover the link between Newcastle and Leek that originally ran up the two roads towards Smallthorne.

By 1820 a new route along Moorland Road had been built in order to improve access from the town centre. The 'Hot Lane Toll-Bar' appears under this name in the 1861 Census with 38 year old Canadian born 'Toll-gate keeper' William Ridgway, his wife Sarah and their five children in residence.

Four Lost Burslem Toll-houses

Tunstall - Bosley etc.

Chell Toll-house
(SJ 877506)
Tunstall - Bosley etc.

A toll-house was positioned on the road from Great Chell to Hanley, probably at its junction with Hamil Road, a route that was turnpiked in 1770 as a branch of the Tunstall to Bosley route.

It appears under the name of the 'Chell Toll-house' in 1871, being occupied at that time by 'toll-collector' Eliza Rathbone her husband John and their two young children.

Holden Hill Toll-house
(SJ 886496)
Tunstall - Bosley etc.

The location of this toll-house was probably to the north of the Sneyd Green Toll-gate, as a later addition to toll-houses on what is now the A5272, at a point where the new road to Endon and Leek crosses.

Built in c.1839 it appears in the 1861 Census returns as 'Holden Gate' with 36 year old 'Collector of Tolls' Elizabeth Poole in residence with her 'miner' husband Thomas and their four children along with three members of the Sawyer family. In 1871 the house is known as the 'Holden Hill Gate House' with the toll-collecting team of Edwin and Susannah Proudlove living there with their two children.

Smallthorn Toll-house, Burslem
(SJ 882502)   'T.G.'
Tunstall - Bosley etc.

Built on High Lane at Nettlebank, near Smallthorn, where the road from Newcastle to Leek crosses the original 1770 turnpike from Great Chell to Hanley, this toll-house appeared as 'Blue Stone' in the 1871 Census.
In 1854 'Coal Higgler' John Oldcott of Burslem was accused of evading tolls by toll-keeper Samuel Perry. The case was contested by the colliery operators Messrs May of Sneyd, who claimed he had driven his ass and cart around the gate over private land and was therefore using a private road exempt from tolls. However, Oldcott was found guilty and fined £2 1s 0d when the actual toll was only 6d.

Sneyd Green Toll-house, Burslem
(SJ 887493)
Tunstall - Bosley etc.

This toll-house was originally built in Sneyd Green at the eastern end of Sneyd Street at or near its junction with the Hanley Road, present day A5272, not long after the Turnpike Act of 1770.
It was positioned on the old Newcastle to Leek route that ran through Cobridge and was also conveniently placed to control part of the Great Chell to Hanley route on the Burslem to Lawton turnpike. The toll-house was occupied in 1871 by 62 year old 'toll-collector' Amy Shufflebottom and her 22 year old son Joseph Vernon.

Brownhills Toll-house, Burslem
(SJ 860503) 'T.G.'
Lawton - Burslem etc.

photo: warrillow collection, keele university library

By 1828 a toll-house operated at Brownhills, on the road to Tunstall at the junction with the road from Longbridge, about a mile north-west of Burslem.

It is recorded in the 1841 Census returns as a toll-bar and weighbridge with 40 year old 'toll-collector' Richard Lawton and his family at the house. In 1871 'Toll-collector' Robert Fletcher had taken over the role, living there with his wife Martha and their two sons Willis and Robert.

This old photograph from the Warrillow Collection at Keele University looks to the south and shows the octagonal-ended toll-house of two storeys with a doorway facing each road and a large toll-board set above the door on the left.

Red Cross Toll-house, Biddulph
(SJ 880567) 'T.G.'
Tunstall - Bosley etc.

Built on the Tunstall Road on the southern outskirts of Biddulph this toll-house controlled the point where the road from Kidsgrove to Biddulph Moor crossed the main route at Red Cross, a point known locally as Knypersley Corner.

The toll-house is shown as a 'T.G.' on early 19th Century OS maps and in 1861 it was occupied by 76 year old 'turnpike toll-collector' John Kirkland and his wife Ann who is also recorded in the role. In 1878 toll-charges in the area were discontinued and the toll-gates removed.

Four Lost Burslem and Tunstall Toll-houses

Lawton - Burslem etc.

High Street Toll-house, Tunstall
(SJ 858517)
Lawton - Burslem etc.

From 1855 a toll-house was positioned at the north end of Joseph Heath's pottery factory in the High Street of Tunstall. It was at or near the junction of King Street, present day Madison Street, and had a side chain.
Very close to the existing Greengates Toll-bar the house in High Street replaced an earlier gate at Colclough Lane and was occupied in 1861 by the toll-collecting team of Ralph and Sarah Delson, living there with their two year old son Ralph junior.

Longbridge Toll-house, Burslem
(SJ 856493)   'T.G.'
Lawton - Burslem etc.

An Act of 1763 permitted a turnpike between Burslem and Lawton in Cheshire, passing through Tunstall, Golden Hill and Kidsgrove. The first toll-house and gate on the route out of Burslem towards Tunstall, now Scotia Road, was built in c.1777 on the north side of Longbridge south of the canal.
It was replaced in 1782 by another to the west of Fowlea Brook at the end of the Longbridge Hays Road on part of the Newcastle to Derby Turnpike and it is this that is shown as a 'T.G.' on early 19th Century OS maps.

Greengates Toll-house, Tunstall
(SJ 859516)
Lawton - Burslem etc.

This toll-house appeared under the name of 'Greengates Street Toll-gate' in the Census returns of 1871, when occupied by 41 year old 'Toll-collector' Eliza Baddeley and her 14 year old daughter Eliza A.

The toll-house was positioned at or near the junction of High Street with Furlong Road about half a mile north of the town. Marked simply as 'Greengate' on early OS maps it marshalled the road into the town from the direction of Chell and Biddulph and may have dated from around 1839 replacing a much older gate at this site.

23 year old 'Toll-collector' Samuel Turner his wife and family were recorded at the house in 1861.

Newcastle Street Toll-house,
(SJ 864496)   **Dale Hall**
Lawton - Burslem etc.

In c.1848 there was another late addition to the toll-houses of Burslem, that at Dale Hall on Newcastle Street (present day B5051) at its junction with Newport Street.
Its aim was to cover the traffic using the Port Vale Wharf. 'Potter and Toll-collector' Thomas Brough and his family were at the house in 1861.

Rookery Toll-house, Kidsgrove
(SJ 836547)
Lawton - Burslem etc.

photo: newcastle under lyme borough council

An Act of 1763 permitted the build of a turnpike road between Burslem and Lawton in Cheshire, the route passing through Kidsgrove along what is now the A50.

An angle fronted two storey brick built toll-house operated somewhere along this road possibly at or near the junction of a minor road leading east to The Rookery.

This old photo shows the traditional style of the house standing as it seems on a hill leading down to a row of other houses. Its position edging into the highway here would have eventually necessitated its demolition to accommodate for widening of the main road.

Pool Fold Toll-house, Biddulph
(approx SJ 888585)
Tunstall - Bosley etc.

The northern approach to Biddulph from Congleton along the present day A527 was controlled by a toll-house at Pool Fold probably where Mow Lane joins from Gillow Heath and continues east into Biddulph Moor, or possibly further north where Grange Road forks right into the village.

The toll-house was recorded in the Census returns of 1871 with 29 year old 'Toll-collector' Clara Stead living there with her newborn daughter Dora. Ten years earlier it appeared as the 'Gillow Toll-gate House', lending some support to the Mow Lane site.

Butts Lane Toll-house, Talke
(SJ 826538)
Tittensor - Talke

The very first Turnpike Act for Staffordshire received Parliamentary approval in 1714 (13 Anne c.22) for the route between the 'Town or village of Tittensor and the most northern part of Talk on the Hill in Butt Lane', a distance of just eight miles.

This classically styled two storey brick building with an angled front was built very much later under an Act of 1823, when the existing course at Hollins in Talke branched into Linley Lane on the turnpike to Cheshire. It stood on the corner of what is now Linley Road at its junction with Congleton Road on the present day A34, about half a mile north of the village.

At the time it was one of four toll-gates to operate in the vicinity of Church Lawton on the Staffordshire-Cheshire border. The toll-house was unfortunately demolished in c.1920 to facilitate road widening at this point, thereby removing one of the county's most significant buildings that had been associated with the turnpike era.

Lower Hartshill Toll-house,
(SJ 857461)   **Penkhull**
Derby - Newcastle under Lyme

Appearing under this name in the 1861 Census this toll-house probably stood where Stoke Old Road joins what is now the A52 Hartshill Road, not far from what was then recorded as Bagshaws Row in the district of Penkhull to the east of Newcastle under Lyme town centre.

Dimsdale Toll-house, Wolstanton
(SJ 841482)   'T.G.'
Tittensor - Talke

Another toll-gate is marked on early 19th Century OS maps as standing near Holditch Mill on the old Tittensor to Talke turnpike, present day A34, south of where the roads now fork left to Nantwich and right to Congleton.

Occupied in 1871 by Northants born 'Toll-collector' Thomas Beasley, his wife and two sons, it was then known as the 'Dimsdale Toll-house'. Many changes have taken place to the road at this point in the 20th Century when no doubt the house was lost to road widening.

Brick Yard Toll-house, Chesterton
(SJ 827497)   'T.G.'
Newcastle under Lyme - Nantwich etc.

photo: newcastle under lyme borough council

Marked as a 'T.G.' on early OS maps this toll-house operated on the Newcastle to Audley turnpike just north of the village of Chesterton in the then hamlet of 'Brick Yard'.

It seems to have been replaced at some point by the nearby Dean's Lane toll-house as it cannot be found in the Census returns between 1841 and 1871.

This old photograph from c.1900 shows the two storey white painted toll-cottage standing right on the edge of what is named as the 'Old Coach Road, Chesterton' positioned on the right before what appears to be a sharp bend.

Village Toll-house, Audley
(SJ 797509)
Newcastle under Lyme - Nantwich

This toll-house stood near enough in the centre of Audley village at the bottom of the Nantwich Road close to where it merges with the road north to Alsager.

It was to the front of what is now known as Bank Cottage and given its rather awkward position the house would have necessitated demolition at some point for road widening.

'Toll-collector' James Johnson was living at the house in 1837 and later in 1861 Matthew Darlington had taken over the role.

135

Dean's Lane Toll-house, Audley
SJ 822506
Newcastle under Lyme - Nantwich etc.

photo: tim jenkinson

The road through Audley was turnpiked in 1766 as a branch of the Newcastle Under Lyme to Nantwich route and this, one of three toll-gates to operate around the village, was built in the fork of Dean's Lane and the main route from Chesterton, now the B5500.

Brick built, as can be seen from the chimneys, the building retains its basic rectangular form with a replacement porch facing the road, but has not been too sympathetically modernised with its new roof, rendered walls and plastic windows.

Appearing under the name 'New Lane, Bignall End' in the Census returns of 1861, it was occupied at that time by 41 year old 'Toll-gate collector' William Frost, his wife Ann and their five children.

Old Peel Toll-house, Audley
(SJ 780503)   'T.G.'
Newcastle under Lyme - Nantwich

The third toll-gate on the road through Audley operated to the west of the village at Old Peel near Shraley Brook. The tall two storey toll-house stood opposite Old Peel Farm at the junction of the road from Halmer End, the present day B5367.

In 1851 'toll-collector' and widow Sarah Gater was at the house with her three children. The toll-house managed to survive at the roadside until as late as 1986 when it was badly damaged by a lorry and had to be demolished.

Clayton Road Toll-booth, Newcastle
(SJ 849456)   'T.G.'
Eccleshall - Newcastle under Lyme

photo: newcastle under lyme borough council

With the appearance of a small single storey lodge type building, this toll-booth once stood on Clayton Road at its junction with Brook Lane and Friarswood Road, little more than half a mile from the centre of Newcastle on the present day A519.

Brick built in c.1867 this old photograph shows what appears to be a small 'gothick' window above a small blocked doorway. Although the site appears as a 'T.G.' on early 19th Century OS maps and the road to Eccleshall was turnpiked in 1823, this particular building would have replaced an older one at this point, but was probably never inhabited.

Brampton Toll-house, Newcastle
(SJ 854470)
Lawton - Burslem etc.

From 1763 the main route from Lawton in Cheshire to Burslem in Stoke on Trent passed through Kidsgrove and Tunstall. A branch from Tunstall came through Trubshaw Cross into Brampton Fields and on to Newcastle Under Lyme.

The Census returns of 1841 place a toll-house somewhere between Queen Street and the then Market Street in Newcastle and it may have stood about a mile or so north of the town in that part known as 'The Brampton'. Living at the house at that time was 'timber merchant' Henry Hall his wife Elizabeth, their five children and three 15 year old boarders.

Four Lost Newcastle under Lyme Toll-houses

Tittensor - Talke

Knapper's Gate Toll-house,
(SJ 859447)   **Trent Vale**
Tittensor - Talke

The road west of Penkhull was part of the first Staffordshire turnpike from Tittensor to Talke in 1714. By 1791 a toll-house had been built at the junction of the road from Penkhull, present day Newcastle Lane, with the main Stafford to Newcastle route at Spittles.

This area became known as 'Knapper's Gate' and in 1851 the toll-house there was occupied by 39 year old 'Toll-gate keeper' George Roberts his 'assistant' daughter Mary and George's sister-in-law 'dress maker' Mary Price. The house was still in evidence in 1878.

Liverpool Rd Toll-house, Shelton
(approx SJ 877457)
Shelton - Cauldon etc.

Said to have been built in Liverpool Road at the junction with Brisley Hill in 1792, when the 'New' road to Shelton joined the old route near Shelton Wharf, this toll-house was occupied in 1871 by 40 year old 'Toll-collector' Henry Kent, his wife Ann, their four children and his 76 year old mother-in-law Elizabeth Edmunds.
Recorded as the 'Liverpool Road Toll-bar' in the Census of that year, it superseded an older toll-gate in the area and stood near Registry Street and the then Lock House on the canal. The toll-house was also still in evidence as late as 1878.

Old Stoke Lane Toll-house,
(SJ 868437)   'T.G.'   **Penkhull**
Tittensor - Talke

A branch off the Tittensor to Talke turnpike was sanctioned under an Act of 1791, running from Trent Vale up to Shelton Wharf in Stoke. A toll-house was built at the junction of Old Stoke Lane (now Trent Valley Road) north of Hanford village at Oak Hill.
It appears in the Census of 1841 as a 'toll-bar' with 35 year old 'turnpike man' John Whittington, his wife and six children in residence. Twenty years later it was recorded as 'Trent Vale Tollgate House', with the 'Tailor and toll-collector' team of William and Lucy Kimber in residence.

Seabridge Toll-house, Newcastle
(SJ 839437)   'T.G.'
Shawbury - Newcastle under Lyme

The road from Newcastle to Market Drayton via Whitmore was first turnpiked in 1769 and by 1820 a toll-house had been built at its junction with Seabridge Lane.

It appeared in the 1851 Census returns as 'The Cloughts, Seabridge', occupied by 34 year old 'toll-collector' and widower William Blackhurst and his older brother 'cordwainer' Thomas. Much widening and realigning of the roads in this area led to the demolition of the house at some point.

Knowl Wall Toll-house, Newcastle
SJ 851393   'T.G.'
Eccleshall - Newcastle under Lyme

photo: tim jenkinson

According to David Vincent (1982), this rather distinctive, and now much modernised, toll-house was originally built in 1825 by Charles Winks, not long after the construction of the road between Newcastle under Lyme and Eccleshall on what is now the A519 near the village of Beech, some four miles south of the town.

Managed by that Trust the house is two storeys high with large bay windows either side of a now blocked central doorway. The 1861 Census returns record it as simply 'Knowlwall, Trentham' with 58 year old 'Garden Labourer and Tollgate Keeper' William Powner at the house, with his wife Myra and their four young children.

Sandyford Toll-house, Swynnerton
(SJ 861364)
Lichfield - Stone etc.

A toll-gate is recorded at Sandyford in the Census returns of 1841 with 15 year old 'Gate keeper' Samuel Turner in residence. By 1861 the 'toll-collector' had become 70 year old Sophia Cartwright.

The toll-house was most likely positioned on what is the present day A51, just north east of the village of Swynnerton, roughly where the M6 motorway passes under at Winghouse Lane. The road here was turnpiked in 1729 as part of the Canwell Gate, Lichfield route via Stone to the county boundary at Woore.

Pepper Street Toll-house, Keele
SJ 802457   'T.G.'
Newcastle under Lyme - Nantwich etc.

photo: tim jenkinson

An Act of 1766 permitted a turnpike between Newcastle under Lyme and Nantwich in Cheshire, passing through Keele and Betley to the county boundary at Gorstyhill along what is now the A525 and then A531. A section of turnpike near Keele was later superseded by a new road to the north.

There was a toll-house about half a mile north west of Keele, on the corner of Old Chapel Close in Station Road. It has been extended to the rear and is of two storeys with a tall brick chimney and projecting octagonal end. In successive Census returns of the 19th Century it appears in 'Pepper Street', the road leading to Silverdale, with long standing 'toll-gate keeper' Francis Proctor and his family in residence in both 1861 and 1871. Retaining the 'Toll-house' name it was on the market in 2010 with an asking price of £250,000.

Deans Gate Toll-house,
(SJ 839456) 'T.G.' **Newcastle**
Newcastle under Lyme - Nantwich

This toll-house also known as the 'Newcastle Gate', operated for the Newcastle to Nantwich Trust on what is now the A525 towards Woore, just over the Cheshire border.

Standing near Thistleberry Avenue in Higherland, the Census of 1861 records 30 year old 'Cordwainer and toll-collector' Jesse Barrow at the house, living there with his wife Eliza and their four children, as well his 'brick maker' brother Henry. Appearing as 'Deans Gate' in that year there is to this day a local garage that retains that name.

Scot Hay Toll-house, Silverdale
SJ 804472
Newcastle under Lyme - Nantwich etc.

photo: tim jenkinson

The road from Newcastle to Nantwich in Cheshire was turnpiked in 1766, with a branch leading back east from Gorstyhill towards the town through Audley, joining the Tittensor-Talke turnpike at Holditch. In between these two turnpikes a number of more rural routes ran through Halmer End and Alsagers Bank, where travellers would attempt to evade the main gates.

Retaining the name 'Toll-house' over the door and positioned at a former cross-roads on the corner of Crackley Lane, near the village of Scot Hay, this now semi-detached brick built house may well have been involved in collecting tolls. The now disused lane leading south links up with the Keele Toll-gate and although the original house looks to have been extended, it retains a small side window along with a curious lean-to section facing onto the road to Alsagers Bank.

Bar Hill Toll-house, Madeley
(SJ 756434)
Newcastle under Lyme - Nantwich

The road between Madeley and Woore in Cheshire was turnpiked under an Act of 1767. The Bar Hill toll-house along with another in the village opposite the Offley Arms Inn at Poolside (SJ 773449) controlled the route here.

Listed as the 'Toll Gate House, Madeley' in the Census of 1871 with 67 year old Harriet Read as the 'toll-collector' the Bar Hill toll-house was probably positioned near the junction of Back Lane leading down into the village of Onneley at the foot of the long Bar Hill.

Lower Toll-house, Wrinehill
SJ 753473   'T.G.'
Newcastle under Lyme - Nantwich etc.

photo: tim jenkinson

Standing about a mile south of Betley, in the village of Wrinehill on a section of road that was built to avoid a steep hill in 1830, this lower toll-gate was positioned at the junction of the Old and New roads beside the Hand and Trumpet public house on what is the present day A531. It replaced an older toll-gate 'T.G.' that stood further south where a road from the west enters (SJ 753471).

Now much extended to the side and rear, the two storey toll-house nevertheless retains its older brick chimneys. Occupied in 1851 by 'toll-gate keeper' Joseph Brassington, his wife Ann and their two sons, it was bought in 1877 at the end of the turnpike era by Lord Wilton.

Upper Toll-house, Wrinehill
(SJ 754469)   'T.G.'
Newcastle under Lyme - Nantwich etc.

The so called 'Wrinehill Upper Gate' on the very southern edge of the village stood close to the junction with a minor road leading west towards Audlem in Cheshire. A painted toll-board listing its charges was stored at the Bluebell Inn until its closure in 2010, when thankfully the artefact was rescued by Newcastle under Lyme Borough Council.

Operating on the Betley to Nantwich route, the site appears as 'T.G.' on early OS maps and a ticket obtained from here passed various other gates in the area including Wrinehill Lower, Keele, Gorstyhill in Cheshire, Audley, Newcastle and a Bailey's Lane Chain. The road was disturnpiked in 1877 upon the closure of the Trust.

Bearstone Road Toll-house, Pipe Gate (Salop)
SJ 738405   'T.G.'
Stafford - Sandon etc.

photo: tim jenkinson

This toll-house, one of two close together, was built in the hamlet of Pipe Gate in Bearstone Road. It is a short distance west of the junction with the main Stone to Nantwich road, present day A51, which had been turnpiked in 1729. It thus controlled access to the 1804 extension to the Stafford to Sandon Trusts's roads through Eccleshall, that joined the main road at nearby Ireland's Cross.

It appears in the Census returns of 1861 simply as 'toll bar' with 53 year old 'toll-collector' William Lawton and his wife Mary living there. Today the toll-house has been very much extended to the rear but retains the name 'Tollgate Cottage'. Now a large two storey building at the road edge, it is perhaps that section of the house nearest to the A51 that appears to be the oldest and probably remaining part of the original building.

Bearstone Toll-house (Salop)
(SJ 725392)   'T.G.'
Stafford - Sandon etc.

Built c.1832 on the turnpike road between Eccleshall and Woore in Shropshire, now the B5026, this toll-house once stood near Bearstone Mill, north of the village of Mucklestone.

Shown as a 'T.G.' on early OS maps the house was occupied in 1861 by 'Agricultural Labourer' James Morrey his wife Hannah and their baby daughter Rebecca. Given its rural position it is unclear why or when the house was demolished.

Four Lost Toll-houses

Roads into Lichfield and Stone

Woore Toll-house (Salop)
(SJ 726435)   'T.G.'
Lichfield - Stone etc.

This toll-house was built near Flash Farm, about a mile north of Woore on the road towards Nantwich in Cheshire, present day A51 London Road.

Appearing as a 'T.G.' on early 19th Century OS maps, it was occupied in 1871 by 56 year old 'Toll-gate keeper' John Jones, his wife Mary and daughter.

Pipe Gate Toll-house (Salop)
(SJ 739406)   'T.G.'
Lichfield - Stone etc.

Not far from the Bearstone Road toll-gate another 'T.G.' is marked on early OS maps near enough in the bend of the main road and close to a now disused and seemingly mostly disappeared lane to Aston.

It stood about a mile and a half south of the village of Woore near the present day Chetwynd Arms public house. As it cannot be located in the Census returns of the mid to late 19th Century it may be that there was just a side gate, here possibly operated by the toll-keeper from the nearby Bearstone Road toll-house.

Whitmore Heath Toll-house
(SJ 795403)   'T.G.'
Shawbury - Newcastle under Lyme etc.

The road between Newcastle Under Lyme and Market Drayton (present day A53) was turnpiked in 1769 and a toll-gate set up at Whitmore Heath, with a toll-house built not long thereafter. It is suggested that the first toll-keeper was a Mr Baldwin, and the village that grew up around the house became known as 'Baldwin's Gate'. To this day 'Tollgate Avenue' survives there and it may be that the house marked as a 'T.G.' on early 19th Century OS maps stood near this junction. In 1871 it was occupied by 55 year old Derbyshire born 'Toll-gate keeper' Ann Starbuck and her two teenage sons. The present day 'Toll-Gate House' in the village is unconnected with the turnpike era.

Stableford Toll-house, Chapel
(SJ 817388)   'T.P.'   **Chorlton**
Lichfield - Stone etc.

A Turnpike Act of 1729 covered a lengthy route from Canwell Gate via Lichfield and Stone north-westward through Stableford to the Cheshire boundary near Woore. Clearly marked as 'Stableford T.P.' on early 19th Century OS maps, a toll-house was built near present day Stableford Railway Bridge in the parish of Chapel Chorlton, at a point where three minor roads join the main highway, now the A51. The toll-house may have become redundant with the coming of the railway and was demolished not long thereafter as it does not appear in Census returns of the mid 19th Century.

5.0 References and Bibliography

Albert, W. 1972 *Turnpike Road System in England 1663-1840* Cambridge

Albutt, M. 1978 *Turnpike Roads of Stafford* Staffordshire Industrial Archaeology Society Journal no 8

Barnett, A. 2003 *Fifteen Miles to Cover* Sedgley Local History Society

Blay, W.F. 1932 *The Story of Walsall Turnpike Roads and Tollgates* J & W Griffin, Walsall

British History Online 2005 *Staffordshire* www.british-history.ac.uk

Brook, F. 1977 *The Industrial Archaeology of the British Isles: 1 The West Midlands* Batsford

Clifford, S. & King, A. (eds) 1993 *Local Distinctiveness* Common Ground

Cruickshank, D. & Wyld, P. 1975 *London: The Art of Georgian Building* Architectural Press

Dodd, A.E. & Dodd, E.M. 1980 *Peakland Roads and Trackways* Moorland Publishing

Dodd, E.M. 1965 *The Blythe Marsh to Thorpe Turnpike* North Staffordshire Journal of Field Studies pp. 1-19

French, A. 2003 *We'm Gooin' to the Arbo'- a history of Walsall Arboretum* Walsall Local History Centre, Walsall Metropolitan Borough Council

Genge, T. 1995 *Sedgley & District* Sutton Publishing

Haines, C. 2000 *Marking The Miles A History of English Milestones* Haines

Hains, B.A. & Horton, A. 1969 *Central England* British Regional Geology HMSO

Harley, J.B. & Oliver, R.R. 1989 *The Old Series Ordnance Survey Maps of England and Wales vol.VII North-central England* Harry Margary Kent

Longton Thomas, A. 1934 *Geographical aspects of the Development of Transport and Communications in North Staffordshire during the 18th Century* Collections for a History of Staffordshire pp. 1-157

Massey, D. 2002 *History of Weston* www.westonstaffs.org.uk

Mowl, T. & Earnshaw, B. 1985 *Trumpet at a Distant Gate* Waterstone

Pawson, E. 1977 *Transport and Economy: The Turnpike Roads of Eighteenth Century Britain* Academic Press

Phillips, A.D.M. & Turton, B.J. 1988 *The Turnpike Network of Staffordshire 1700-1840: An Introduction and Handlist of Turnpike Acts* Collections for a History of Staffordshire, 4th Series Volume 13 pp. 61-118

Searle, M. 1930 *Turnpikes and Toll-bars* Hutchinson

Serjeant, W.R. & Penrose, D.G. (eds) 1973 *Suffolk Turnpikes* E Suffolk RO

Sherlock, R. 1976 *The Industrial Archaeology of Staffordshire* David & Charles

Smith, P. 1970 *The Turnpike Age* Luton Museum and Art Gallery

Speake, R. (ed) 1974 *The Old Road to Endon* Keele University

Vincent, D. 1982 *Victorian Eccleshall* Brookes Ltd, Hanley

Wolverhampton Journal 1905 *Old Toll Gates*

Wright, G.N. 1992 *Turnpike Roads* Shire

Acknowledgements:

Marie Marriott: For her great help with photographs of toll-houses in the areas of Walsall and Lichfield

Chris Copp: For his consistent help and advice on old photographs from various Staffordshire archives that have greatly complemented the content of this book.

George Blackham: For his help with compiling the information and unravelling the complicated histories and locations of the various toll-houses of the Sedgley district

Ann Jenkinson: For her unwavering support in the investigation of Census records in the county that have revealed several additional sites of toll-houses and their inhabitants from the mid 19th Century.

Various archive photos appear in the book reproduced with the kind permission of:

Birmingham Libraries and Archives
Darlaston Local History Group
Keele University Library
Museum of Cannock Chase
Newcastle under Lyme Borough Council
Staffordshire Arts and Museum Service
Staffordshire Record Office
Tamworth Castle
Walsall Local History Centre
William Salt Library
Wolverhampton Archives and Local Studies

Of Related Interest

The Toll-houses of Cornwall
Patrick Taylor   2001   £7.95
ISBN 0 902660 29 2   iv+80pp
Federation of Old Cornwall Societies

A comprehensive survey of the toll-houses of Cornwall, dating mainly from the 18th and 19th Centuries.

Illustrated with an extensive gazetteer, this was the first in a series that plans to cover the entire country.

"A useful detailed county study with photographs of high quality"
Industrial Archaeology Review

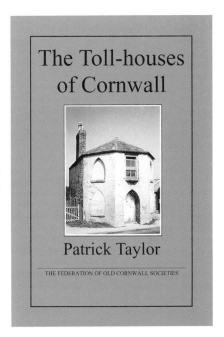

The Toll-houses of South Devon
Tim Jenkinson & Patrick Taylor
Polystar Press   2009   £8.95
ISBN 978 1 907154 01 0   iv+120pp

A comprehensive survey of the toll-houses of South Devon, dating mainly from the 18th and 19th Centuries.

Illustrated with an extensive gazetteer, the first of two volumes covering a large county rich with turnpike remains.

"The book has quality and is attractively presented .... packed with excellent photographs, old and new"
The Milestone Society Newsletter

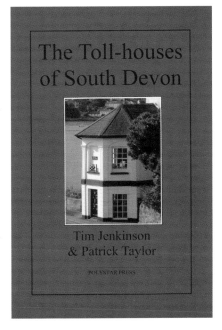

The Toll-houses of Norfolk
Patrick Taylor   2009   £7.95
ISBN 978 1 907154 02 7   iv+76pp
Polystar Press

Research interrupted by the Norwich Library fire finally resumed and brought to publication.

Essentially the same format as the Suffolk volume: history of the turnpike roads, detailed gazetteer of the county plus an appendix on the impostors.

"timely and important records of those that survive and also those - sadly the majority - that have been lost"
Norfolk Industrial Archaeology Soc.

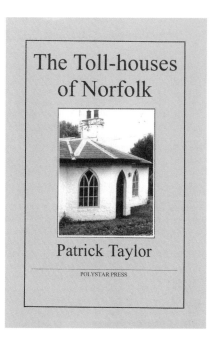

The Toll-houses of Suffolk
Patrick Taylor   2009   £7.95
ISBN 978 1 907154 00 3   iv+84pp
Polystar Press

A comprehensive survey of the toll-houses of Suffolk, dating mainly from the 18th and 19th Centuries.

Illustrated with an extensive gazetteer, and an appendix covering buildings that might be mistaken for toll-houses.

"This useful study of an under-valued and threatened building type is therefore to be welcomed"
Suffolk Historic Buildings Group

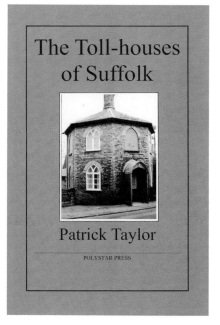